Tried, Tested *and* True

POETS

from

ACROSS *the* GLOBE

❧ RENEE' DRUMMOND-BROWN ❧
RENEE'S POEMS WITH WINGS ARE WORDS IN FLIGHT

AuthorHouse™
1663 Liberty Drive
Bloomington, IN 47403
www.authorhouse.com
Phone: 1 (800) 839-8640

Published by AuthorHouse 12/06/2017

ISBN: 978-1-5462-0491-6 (sc)
ISBN: 978-1-5462-0493-0 (hc)
ISBN: 978-1-5462-0492-3 (e)

Library of Congress Control Number: 2017913694

Print information available on the last page.

Scripture quotations marked KJV are from the Holy Bible, King James Version (Authorized Version). First published in 1611. Quoted from the KJV Classic Reference Bible, Copyright@1983 by The Zondervan Corporation.

Any people depicted in stock imagery provided by Thinkstock are models,
and such images are being used for illustrative purposes only.
Certain stock imagery © Thinkstock.

This book is printed on acid-free paper.

authorHOUSE®

TRIED, TESTED AND TRUE POETS FROM ACROSS THE GLOBE

Renee's Poems with Wings are Words in Flight
"INDESCRIBABLE POETRY
May God use you as a messenger
to fulfill all of His great works.
Speak,
teach,
reach
every mind;
for these are trying times.
Creativity of words of the art you bring to us
are like
a painted picture
being told
of the mystery of our history.
Thanks for your gift
Love Mom"

(Barbara Ann Drummond)

Affirmation

"Iron sharpeneth iron;
so a man sharpeneth
the countenance of his friend"
(Proverbs 27:17 KJV.)

TRIED, TESTED AND TRUE POETS FROM ACROSS THE GLOBE

CONTENTS

vii

DEDICATED

Around The World In 180 Poems!

By: Author Renee' Drummond-Brown

(Renee's Poems with Wings are Words in Flight!)

Round an' round
we go…
Where
'our'
21st century
poetic thoughts
stop;
some of the following
Poets
have
gone
on
long
before.

ROLL CALL:

Phillis Wheatley
William Wordsworth
William Shakespeare
Oscar Wilde
Emily Dickinson
Maya Angelou
Rabindranath Tagore
Robert Frost
Langston Hughes
Watt Whitman
Shel Silverstein

William Blake

Sylvia Plath

Pablo Neruda

William Butler Yeats

Alfred, Lord Tennyson

Rudyard Kipling

Tupac Shakur

Edward Estlin (E.E.) Cummings

Charles Bukowski

Muhammad Ali

Sandra Cisneros

Henry Wadsworth Longfellow

Alice Walker

Sarojini Naidu

Billy Collins

Christina Rossetti

Carol Ann Duffy

Edgar Allan Poe

John Donne

Ralph Waldo Emerson

Nikki Giovanni

John Keats

Raymond Carver

Ogden Nash

Lewis Carroll

Thomas Hardy

Mark Twain

Spike Milligan

Carl Sandburg
Anne Sexton
Alexander Pushkin
Percy Bysshe Shelly
Henry David Thoreau
Elizabeth Barrett Browning
Roger McGough
Victor Hugo
Sara Teasdale
George Gordon Byron
Gary Soto
Thunchaththu Ramanujan Ezhuthachan

Poet Laureate Renee' B. Drummond-Brown (I've been here before).

Dedicated to: POETRY IS THE ESSENCE OF THINGS HOPED FOR.

A B.A.D. Poem

Who Blows There?

By: Author Renee' Drummond-Brown

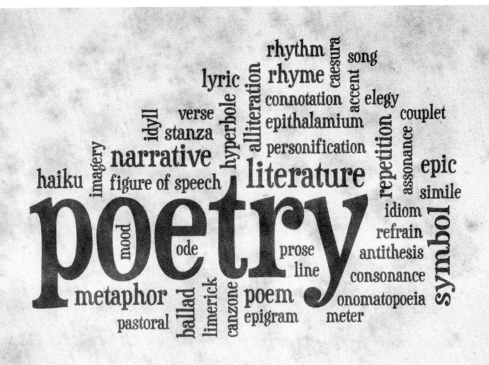

Beneath
the Valley
lows
and/or
Mountaintop highs
for sure.

Slowly
but
surely;
dropping
'our'
prolific
prose
as
we soar
to
an' fro
full circle
across
the globe.

We 'SPIT'
words
of wisdom
AS KNOWN AS
wisdom prose.
Who blows there?

Only 'our'
bad
poetry knows.
Yeah
it knows
for sure;
'OUR'
hot air.

Dedicated to:

The poets/poetess across the globe who contributed in this book.
Thank you my friends for sharing your INK.

A B.A.D. Poem

PROLOGUE

"Tried, Tested and True Poets from Across the Globe"
By: Author Renee' Drummond-Brown

'TRIED'
it all.
Annoyed
with self.
Vexed
by games,
exasperated
one's call.
Provoked
by this thang
called poetry.
Yeah,
You guessed it
Shakespeare
for us
rang.
Sonnets

SUMMONED
OUR
NAMES

'TESTED'
again;
you guessed it;
across
the globe.
Verified
an'
confirmed.
Established.
Recognized.
AND YES
'ev'n'
well-known.
Reputable
non
traditional.
Conventional;
who
could've known?

To be
or
not to be
or
be to not
or
be to experienced
to
write
the world
'sum'
poetic
blues;
'fo' 'sho'.

'TRUE'
our literature
comes correct.
Accurate prose
again,
you guessed…
it;

actual
factual
real
an'
definite
genuine
realistic
fiction
nonfiction
our poetry
is
concrete
AND YES
truth be told;
authentic
around the world
in 180 poems!

Dedicated to:
Around the world in 180 poems and the authors who made this book happen!
THANK YOU ALL.

A B.A.D. Poem

OTHER BOOKS BY RENEE' DRUMMOND-BROWN

~A B.A.D. Poem

~The Power of the Pen

~SOLD: TO THE HIGHEST BIDDER

~RENEE'S POEMS WITH WINGS ARE WORDS IN FLIGHT-I'll Write Our Wrongs!

~Renee's Poems with Wings are Words in Flight (e-Book)

"I've never seen anyone who can yield their words as with a sword.

You are a literary genius whose work is phenomenal...

every time I read one of your masterpieces

I think to myself,

"it can't get any better than this"... and then you do it again,

and again and again.

You have me awestruck!"

(Denise Boozer).

TRIED, TESTED AND TRUE POETS FROM ACROSS THE GLOBE

ACKNOWLEDGMENT

I met Renee' Drummond-Brown going on three years ago in my online Facebook Poetry Forum Page, POTPOURRI POETS/ARTISTS WRITING COMMUNITY. As a Publisher of my own company, (WILDIFRE PUBLICATIONS), I am always seeking out new talent. All it took was ONE POEM I read of Renee's and I thought to myself: now here is a writer who can be a role model not only to Writers like herself, but the populace in general, for her strength and power of the pen is beyond just a gesture of hidden talent. Words written with such innate passion that it literally jumps off the page with a life of its own, outright pure and simple.

Each Masterful and heartfelt stanza manifests emotions that perhaps you tucked away deeply for years and was afraid to cut it loose. Surely such persuasive sincerity the entire world relishes secretly as well, but individually or as a group unit, all don't quite know how to structure or discipline such razor sharp-edges of faith, reluctant to utter such questioning of our world and the things that happen to us. In Renee's world, blatant dishonesty and prejudice NEEDS TO BE REPLACED with love, harmony, light, respect, embracing all formats of diversity. Before venturing out into the Universe with such fervor, first we must learn to love and believe in ourselves and the rest will fall into place. We need to stop complaining and get into a viable solution, and miraculously, Renee's poetry shows the way to do that if you read in-between the lines. Upon reading her, I was encouraged to get up and do something about our state of affairs and not just lay on the couch and let someone else do it.... it's just the way she presents her phraseology that penetrates the skin and stays there and does not let us lay back down .... the world will listen more to a whisper than a scream and it takes REAL TALENT to whisper a calling than to yell for a call to arms.

What is it about this Author that we love? Love her for that big Heart and powerful words; we love her too because she's everyone's sister, she's there for you, she speaks for YOU, and she speaks it well, poetically, and strongly, without trepidation, inhibition or ridicule because she's a dedicated and intense but self-assured woman and believes in us and believes enough in HERSELF, which makes it easy to respect this Remarkable Writer!!!

A Poet of such magnitude of Strength and Conviction comes rarely our way and when it does, consider it as gift from the Poetic Gods above. She speaks with honor, speaks the same language as one's shy heart and Soul .... her words bestowing empowerment and MEANING to those who feel voiceless or repressed for reasons of their own .... I feel I can relax knowing someone out there as Prolific as Renee' can say these things critical to the human condition, valid to the state of societal affairs and injustices; write those flaming words, emancipate the controlled disparity in a world gone haywire. Without doubt, Renee' is a breed of literary healing in some respects; the elixir of her compelling body of works speaks volumes at a time when many feel bare to the bone. I haven't the talent to utter or manifest what she effortlessly brings forth in each composition... springing to life universal moralistic views, anger towards a world often Unjust, bringing awareness to those ignoring the evidence before them. She hopes to wake up the "dead" who are blindly convinced that nothing will ever change so why bother to fight? Renee' reminds us there is something to fight for, we must not stand still.

It seems our own quiet Spirits rise to meet the POUNDING of hers to create a Union that embraces multiplicity of the human condition, both past and future, and equality as it should have been throughout history and even now, as she burns the pages with intelligent and empathetic gentleness. What is also amazing in the journey of Renee's books is the historical features she refers to; you can take the trip back in time to the 19th century and become that Slave on the Chop Block being sold like livestock to the highest bidder; all the way into our current century where prejudice still abounds and is taken out on our youth or instigated by youth in dense places such as malls, football games, theaters, parties, lounges.

Renee' takes Poetry to a whole new level, and you will love her style of keeping it real, bringing history into the light to relive those tumultuous years of struggle and bias, and the slow progress seen today of acceptance of change and the snail-paced endeavors to disown prejudices and hate. Renee', in the rarity and uniqueness she brings to the table, flings her poetic songs in a way that comes off as a fiery whisper but that is often what it takes to wake up a pandemonious world and she pulls it off like no one else has the audacity or stamina to do. We need more poets like Renee' but we are blessed at least to have ONE who's making a difference. It only takes one erratic move in topography to cause an Avalanche. And that's what Renee' Drummond-Brown is doing, one word, one phrase, one paragraph stanza, at a time.

-THE WILDFIRE PUBLICATIONS
Susan Joyner-Stumpf, FOUNDER/President

Renee' Dummond-Brown is a major contributor to Raven Cage Zine, a poetry and prose Ezine. Her prose gives the magazine the diversity it is built upon. Her use of slang, or as I lovingly call it, straight talking street talk is always welcome by Raven Cage.

-JERRY LANGDON
Editor of Raven Cage Zine

Renee' Drummond-Brown was one, and still is a member of my Facebook poetry group, *Contemporary Poets, Their Works, Current Poetry Projects, News, and Links* with over 13,300 members as of this date: https://www.facebook.com/groups/807679459328998/. As an internationally published poet in 33 countries, editor of 10 poetry sites, and publisher, at this point in my life helping others I believe in, is as important to me as establishing my own poetic legacy to leave behind. Often a poet with potential only needs someone to have faith in them, to help with confidence, give them a jump-start, some take the bait, and some do not. Renee' Drummond-Brown was one of those members who listened and said, "I can do this!" Within two years, Renee' has established herself as a poet of merit fire in flames by her own desire to leave a mark in her life. I recently published Renee' in my successful selling poetry anthology Dandelion in a Vase of Roses: http://www.amazon.com/dp/1545352089. Two of her stellar poems "Sing a Song," and "Impolite Wine" found there. It is my joy to embrace this budding of a rose, this new poetic star.

-MICHAEL LEE JOHNSON
Contemporary Poets, Their Works, Current Poetry Projects, News, and Links

All good and perfect gifts come from God. Renee' Drummond-Brown's prose continues to be an example of that gift...only God given and God inspired. Keep writing to right the many ills of society.

-JUDITH HAMPTON THOMPSON
Publisher, Metro Gazette Publishing Company, Inc.

"Words cannot express how much I admire and love Renee' Drummond-Brown's poems. They are so uplifting and speaks truth in every one. I am just in awe!"

-RUTHA MAE HARRIS OF ALBANY, GA.,
Original Freedom Singer and Civil Rights Activist

Renee' Drummond-Brown's book was nominated as the "Poetry Book of the Year." I read selections and backed the evaluator of her book. Buy it and you will not be sorry. In fact your will be pleased, and thank me for recommending it..."

-HALIF KHALIF KHALIFAH
PUBLISHED BLACK WRITERS ON FACE BOOK

For Master poet Renee' Drummond Brown to undertake the generous act of publishing book honoring other poets and include me among them, is unexpected honor that I immensely appreciated. I am thankful to be in the company of so many distinguished literati.

-ELIZABETH ASCHE DOUGLAS

Mom, you are one of the most powerful, creative, and gifted writers of today. It is amazing how you have created yet another masterpiece that is part of a collection of books that captures the spirit inside of you to educate and empower us in everything from scripture to civil rights to even addressing the issues among the youth today. Your style of writing is beyond description, vivid imagery and compelling words putting us in that time, place, struggle, or situation. Your talents are not only on the level of some of the greatest writers of all time, but they are also in an untouchable category of their own. Last, my family and I thank you so much for writing the beautiful poem in loving memory of our beloved Clarese Renee' White and publishing it in this book. Clarese's spirit could not have been described more perfectly; her remembrance will forever be maintained. Keep on blessing, motivating, and uniting us with your brilliant works. I love you dearly.

-SANESE WHITE-BROWN, M.S.

It started with a vision which led to the cultivation of literary prose. She nurtured her vision through sleepless nights. The sweat from her brow provided the water as her hands penned literary works which toiled the soil to make way for fertile ground. On this ground she would empower people globally, and give voice to today's poets. She is a seed. It is for this reason that Renee's words with wings have taken flight and she is recognized and respected across the globe. Renee' Drummond-Brown is not only an Author she is a torch bearer who inspires others to dream in color.

You are an inspiration Auntie Renee'

-Dr. Terri Drummond

She's managed to do it once again. Another amazing piece of literary work to add to her extensive collection. I wish you continued success in all your endeavors because I know this book will be a hit. I Love you mom.

-Cardell Nino Brown Jr., B.A.

Words cannot describe how proud I am of my mother, Reneé Drummond-Brown, and her collection of books. Keep on writing, empowering, and being an inspiration to our family, friends, and others who enjoy your writing prose. You are a role model to those young, old and anything in between. You deserve everything that is coming your way (and then some) because you sacrificed so much for your family and many others. Renee's Poems with Wings are Words in Flight cannot be tamed. Continue to soar mom, I love you.

-Dr. Renee' Barbara-Ann Brown

I am extremely proud of my mother, Renee' Drummond-Brown's body of literary works, seen across the globe. I love you mom…forever your "Raven Blackbird."

-Raven Chardell Brown, B.A.

AUTHOR NANCY NDEKE SALUTATIONS TO
AUTHOR RENEE' DRUMMOND-BROWN'S WRITING PROSE

"Whoa!!!!!
The best of the best.... A true treatise on social, cultural, religious, politik and then SOME more.
My sister you are gifted, why lie!!!
Shine mine dear sister
You speak
To
Situations and
Conditions and
Our hearts and
Minds
Generation's
Our separations
Our forwards
Our backwards
And our Limbo
Oooh, how so apt
You say it dear
As a mother
As a citizen
As an artist
As one whose eye
Scans society

Without condemnation
Asks as you tell
Demands as you give
The voice of emotions
Drilling for the truth
When
Did the rain
Start beating us.
Lol!!!
Awesome!!!!!"

-AUTHOR NANCY NDEKE, KENYA, NAIROBI

OMG!!!!!
My, oh my?
You know, I have been
Reading your works but its
This last hour I realized
Yours is not just poesy.
It's a mission in poesy
A teaching
A preaching
A calling
Sooo unique
But readily
Touching base
With every word
Every line
Beyond the immediate
To the broad
The past
Present
Continuum
With a soul search pique

Absolutely amazing and
Godly
Ordained
Persuaded by a hand
That calls for balance
In love, kindness
Social responsibility
And ownership
Of our wrongs
To right them
And calling gospel
And history
To bear this future
Witness.

WOW!!!"

-Author Nancy Ndeke, Kenya, Nairobi

A special thank you to:

-Mr. Richard J. Muzzey **of** Wonday Portrait Studio & Location Photography,
for the photographic gifts and talents contributed to my book. www.wondayportraitstudio.com

-Mr. Tim Cobb of TNT Photography, for the photographic gifts and talents contributed to my book. tnt-photo.com

-Mr. Anthony Antonelli and Dr. Renee' Barbara-Ann Brown for the contributed You Tube videography.

-Wildfire Publications Magazine, Susan Joyner-Stumpf, President and Deborah Brooks Langford, Executive Vice President.

-Jerry Langdon, Editor of Raven Cage Zine

-Michael Lee Johnson, Chief-in-Editor, Contemporary Poets, Their Works, Current Poetry Projects, News, and Links

-Judith Hampton Thompson, Publisher, Metro Gazette Publishing Company, Inc.

-Rutha Mae Harris of Albany, GA., Original Freedom Singer and Civil Rights Activist

-Elizabeth Asche Douglas, Owner/Principal Artist at Douglas Art Gallery

-Author Nancy Ndeke, Kenya, Nairobi

-A heartfelt thank you to all of the poets across the globe who contributed their poetic voices through their prolific prose within this book.

ACKNOWLEDGEMENTS

PHILLIS WHEATLEY
By: Author Renee' Drummond-Brown

Phillis Wheatley,
how dare you
DREAM
of
a colored,
gal
like me,
born
of the
60's;
PENNING
the
'dag' on 'thang'
in
the
21st
century.

Now,
like you,
DR. MAYA ANGELOU
and

ALICE WALKER
TOO;
NOT 'IF'
BUT
'WHEN',
I'm looooooong
'outta'
sight;
I
CHARGE
the next
colored gal,
with
"RENEE'S POEMS WITH WINGS ARE WORDS IN FLIGHT!"
Fly Blackbird(s) Fly
an' we'll
'neva'
'eva'
forsaken you
in the
still
of your
penning
night(s).

Dedicated to: POETRY AT ITS FINEST HOUR

A B.A.D. Poem

RENEE'S QUOTES:

"As my wings take flight, unlike the Raven; I won't forget to land"

"Around the world in 180 poems!"

*"Blood is thicker than water, or so they say.
Funny how water supported me
along life's journey way"*

"Deep ink really thinks"

"Don't come correct; come poetic"

"Great pens INK alike"

"I never knew 'IT' till then; but thank you Father, for the Power in my pen"

"If 'ya'll' ain't 'gonna' poetically flow; take your 'dead' brains home"

"Ignorance starts at home; then goes abroad"

"It's WONDERFUL being peculiar; didn't always think so growing up!"

"ONE'S wings can't carry everyONE"

"Poetry is not about how one feels, but rather, what their pen thINKS"

"STILL I WRITE, I WRITE, I'LL WRITE"

"The Pens come out at night"

"There's power in my pen; cause 'HE' said so."

"To be a Scholar, you must know Scholars, to be dumb; you must know dummies"

"To rid a fool; one must act one"

"Trouble in my way; I 'gotta' SHINE 'sumtimes'

"What 'reign' God showers upon us"

"When you shut your mouth; you begin to hear their thoughts"

"When touching God's keys; I never know where 'His' poetry is going to drive me"

"There's Power in my pen; signed Poet Laureate, Renee' B. Drummond-Brown"

2 to The Head 1 to The Chest

By: Author Renee' Drummond-Brown

My pen's
bad
as can be.
Shoots
no blanks.
Prolific
on them
scenes.
She thINKS
2 to
the head.
1 to
the chest;
no questions asked.
Picture this:
straight up…
WILD WILD WEST!

Dedicated: *Dead is dead is dead.*

A B.A.D. Poem

'A'

By: Author Renee' Drummond-Brown

Some say
I'm
'A'
first.
Others say
I'm
'A'
last.
Some say
I'm
wicked.
Others
might say
I
'gotta'
grade
'A'
class.

Some say
I'm
'A'
beast.
Others
might say
I'm
'A'
tree.
Some say
I'm
'A'
genius
with the
poetic lines
I 'sang'
for free.

But…
I say,
long as
I got
poetry
I'm
just
'A'

Dedicated to: *I did it my way.*

A B.A.D. Poem

A first love is just luv

By: Author Renee' Drummond-Brown

Romeo and Juliet
will share
true-love.
A kiss is just a kiss.
Romeo and Juliet
will never
forget.
A death is just a death.
Romeo and Juliet
will painfully
regret.

Dedicated to: *First true-luv.*
A B.A.D. Poem

A HARD HEAD MAKES A SOFT BEHIND

By: Author Renee' Drummond-Brown

Hairdressing Salon

As a baby girl
Momma, watched you grow.
She said,
slow down
my child;
you ain't
got
nowhere
fast to go!

As a lil' girl
she played
dress up
each
and every-day;
'tryin'
Momma's
lipstick, dresses
an'
high heels on.
'Movin' her body seductively;
like a grown up
woman would,
'fo' real.
Momma watched
her growth,
and said,
"slow down
my child;

you ain't
got
nowhere
fast to go!"

As a child,
Momma even seen
her attraction
to men,
an' said,
"never sit on a man's lap,
shut your legs
when wearing
a dress,
and never
ever
talk back."
Momma, watched you growing
with a keen eye
but,
somehow knew
and knowing
you
were destined
to grow up
VERY FAST
and meet
and greet,

the troubles
that awaited you,
at last!!!

As a teenage girl,
Momma can't tell you
A THING.
So,
you took
to
a fast paced
world
and did your own
grown up 'THANGS'!
'Walkin' round
half-naked,
'takin' selfies
of self.
Respect
for no-one;
including thyself.
Fast life,
gone
downstream,
shipwrecked.
'Takin' men
on a swirl;
or so
you thought.

Got out of them
'ev'rythang' you could.
Jokes
on you 'BABY!
You ain't hardly using them; 'inna' man's
GREAT BIG world,
they're using your 'bod' for 'FREE'
'fo' 'sho'.
Momma, watched
an' 'UNKNOWN CHILD' grown.
She said,
WITH A BROKEN HEART,
slow down
child;
you ain't
hardly got
nowhere fast
to go!

As a young woman
emerged;
bags under her eyes,
lines in her arms.
Life begins to show.
'Cept',
she don't even know,
let lone,
own it.

And poor Momma,
who watched her grown.
AIN'T ALIVE NO-MORE
to say,
"slow down
my child;
you ain't
got
nowhere 'ELSE' fast to go!"

AND NOW
YOU'RE
OUT THERE
'ALL ALONE'.
WITH EVERYWHERE FAST
TO GO;
AS YOU ROAM
TO AN' FRO
WITH
TOM,
DICK,
HARRY
AND THEM
UNKNOWN
JOE'S.

He who 'IZ' without sin;
let 'THEM'

cast 'HER' a stone….
NOT NAIR ONE OF US HAVE ROCKS IN OUR HANDS
TO THROW AT HER
OR
THEM JOE'S!!!
JUST SHUT UP
AND LET GOD DO WHAT HE DO
TO WORK ON HER!
WHILE YOU AT IT
ASK 'HIM'
TO WORK ON YOUR 'DUNG' TOO.

Dedicated to: *Whomever, this poem is written for 'baby girl' take heed: get the help that you need and 'PLEASE' slow down. The world is not against you…YOU ARE IMPORTANT, AND YOU DO MATTER TO THE FATHER WHO ART IN HEAVEN. TRY GOD. You've tried everything else.*

A B.A.D. Poem

A Heart Broken Soul

By: Author Renee' Drummond-Brown

She
gave 'em'
her all.
It
must've
'NOT'
been enough.
They gave her
their minds
an'
then 'sum'
supplementary
stuff.

She inhales
it
'ALL'
and
exhales
the lows.

She rented
a heart
with
a broken
soul.

But…
He
knows
for sure.

He
certainly
knows.

Dedicated to: *It's just emotions taken us 'ov'r'.*

A B.A.D. Poem

A Man's 'BEST' Friend

By: Author Renee' Drummond-Brown

He treated
her
like
a dog.
His friend
comes along;
treats her
like
'a' god.

He treated her
like scum
an' dirt.
his friend
comes along
an'
'SEES'
her worth.

He don't
'SEE'
the beauty
within her.
His friend
comes along
and defines
her growth,

an'
made her
know
she's yet
to be
unearthed.

He beats his baby
'outta' her.
His friend
comes along
an' replenishes
her
earth.
Guess who's
with
the friend
and
guess who's
now hurt?

Dedicated to: *A man's best friend 'IZ' his 'dawg'.*

A B.A.D. Poem

Ain't

By: Author Renee' Drummond-Brown

Ain't
'gonna' give up!
Ain't
gone give in!
Ain't
'gonna' give out!
Ain't
gone 'NEVA'
betray
a friend!

Dedicated to: *Ain't got 'nothin' but 'luv' to give.*

A B.A.D. Poem

Ain't Had

By: Author Renee' Drummond-Brown

Ain't had
no joy.
Ain't had
no fun.
Ain't had
no seasons
in
The Son.

We had
hate
and pride
and drowned
before
the tide.

Dedicated: SOS.

A B.A.D. Poem

Aint No 'Sangin' In the Rain

By: Author Renee' Drummond-Brown

Father,
'why'd' you call
'her'
Bernard home,
an' leave
her
here,
all alone
to witness,
a grave filled,
headstone?
Filled with tears,
misery
and strife;
its not
suppose to be him.
She was more
than
his wife.

Therefore,
I'll flood
the
thundering reign(s).
Ain't no 'sonshine'
where he's gone;
aint no 'sangin'
in the rain.
Until,
their quiet storm(s)
meet again.

Dedicated to: *I'll 'sang' a song for you, Aunt Christine Drummond.*

ALL

By: Author Renee' Drummond-Brown

He gave her
his
all.
She
took advantage.
Bought him out;
at malls.
'USED' up
his
credit cards.
Took him
for broke;
she's
the real deal.
Lest
he fall.

Oh but…
PRIDE;
she
showed herself
to her.
Like a ditch
dug
for two.
…..And when she fell;
she fell hard.
One grave marked
her name.
The other…..
…..Well
unquestionably,
stole back
her
corroded things!

Dedicated to: *Manipulators AKA Users.*

A B.A.D. Poem

All Our Life: We 'Gotta' Fight!

By: Author Renee' Drummond-Brown

All our life we 'gotta' fight.
We 'gotta' fight
to be black.
We 'gotta' fight
to be right.
We 'gotta' fight through the day.
We 'gotta' fight throughout our night(s).
We 'gotta' fight
for
the color of our skin;
don't matter
red
yellow
black
and/or
the half breed within.
We 'gotta' fight our black men.
We 'gotta' fight his children.
We 'gotta' fight the white man.
We 'gotta' fight his woman.
We 'gotta' fight our families
an'
the nonsense they 'brang'!
We 'gotta' fight self
an'
the demons within.
We 'gotta' fight the system.
We 'gotta' fight for education.

We 'gotta' fight against retaliation.
We 'gotta' fight the President of our Nation(s).
We 'gotta' fight for our Salvation.
We 'gotta' fight Satan,
with
the good fight;
in addition,
them haters!
We 'gotta' fight against deprivation
We 'gotta' fight against discrimination
We 'gotta' fight 'for' our children
We 'gotta' fight 'for' our men
We 'gotta' fight for justice
An' do it
without
wearing a grin!

'ALL' 'WE' 'KNOW'
is to fight them;
and in
'ALL' our fighting
we forgot;
how to be
a woman?

Dedicated to: *Watch,* **'FIGHT'** *and pray!!!*

A B.A.D. Poem

An Elephant in the Room

By: Author Renee' Drummond-Brown

A pink elephant in the room.
Is obviously present, nonetheless metaphorically doomed.
An issue none wants to discuss.
A challenge beyond what appears true.

Dedicated to: *To be or not to be is the question an elephant in the room would ask of thee?*

A B.A.D. Poem

Anew

By: Author Renee' Drummond-Brown

Michael, started
with
that
man in the mirror.
You kids today
must
start
with your heart.
Mike, tried
to get it right,
while
he had
the time.
But my children,
your heart
controls
the mind.

You can't get it right
not in
this lifetime
cause
your strengths
bank on
borrowed time.

But…
The Father,
can
fix your mind,
mend
your heart,
reset
your clock back
to
its
original start.

Dedicated to: *Change your ways.*

A B.A.D. Poem

Baby

By: Author Renee' Drummond-Brown

Baby,
what we 'gone' do?
I'm 'feedin'
for two.
Our parents,
don't know
bout
me an' you.
You're white
as
the day is long.
I'm black
as the night.
Are we so wrong?
Or
are they right?

Baby,
what we 'gone' do
bout us
3
???

Dedicated to: *How far long are you?*

A B.A.D. Poem

BACK-STABBERS

By: Author Renee' Drummond-Brown

Her
'BEST' friend
told her
'ev'rythang'
she needed
to know;
to be

rid of him
' fo' sho!!!

She said
"he's a liar and a cheat."
She said
"he ain't worth the shoes on your precious feet."
She said
"he's no good for you"
She said
"call it quits 'cos' technically you've been through!"
She 'ev'n' said
"he's got 'sum'
babies on the way."

In hindsight;
revisiting
'THAT'
very day
an' now know
what
she didn't
yesterday.
'TWAS' sistah gal;

'THE 'WANNABE' OTHER WOMAN'
'tellin' her
all them
foul thangs
'THAT'
wasn't true.
Come to find out
he was
ever
so faithful to you.

LESSON 101:
BACK-STABBERS
'DO'
smile in your face
'WHILE PLANNING'
to take
your place.

Dedicated to: *'ALWAYS' keep your enemies 'CLOSER' than family and friends!*

A B.A.D. Poem

ROMEO DELLA VALLE

Biography

Born in the Caribbean island of Santo Domingo, Dominican Republic, from a Dominican mother and an Italian father, I was brought to New York City at a very young age (as a teenager) and pursued my education here to later graduating at the University of New York City, and obtaining the BA (Bachelor Degree) in Arts. Due to my language, at the beginning, I was forced to place emphasis on my reading and writing skills to be able to communicate in a very effective way. While at Baruch College (C.U.N.Y.), I enrolled in the journalism course which I passed with a high mark, then, I started to write short articles and poems in English and Spanish as well for the student newspaper!

I started to enjoy arts and writing so much that I enrolled also in the Arts Students League of New York where I took classes on Oil Painting for a few years. I did quite a few painting on oil: Still Life, Portrays and Landscapes which now are privately owned by a dear friend named Monica Kenney who lives in Germany. At that time, I joined the first Poetry Group: Poemhunter.com where I have posted around 400 poems until I joined Facebook and other poetry groups. I also created the poetry groups: Show World Poetry, The Challenge-Ang Paghamon, Mi Rincon Poetico (Spanish) and Just Beautiful Quotes and Images. As a poet, I have traveled to the Philippines twice for Poetry Events where I received recognitions as a poet

and as Keynote Speaker at the University of Everga, Quezon, Philippines. Presently, I am still living in New York City and working in the publication of my first poetry book. To me, poetry is in everything, even in the air that I breathe.

BACK TO THE FUTURE

By: Author Romeo Della Valle

When life was at ease
And nature undisturbed
Without electronic eyes
Or any modern device
tracking down
Our every moves
But now only the wind
Freely moves instead!

Pure air filling our lungs
And crystal clear water
Calming down our thirst,
When material things
Were the last result
But life was always first!

No bird machines
Polluting the skies
Or twisted philosophy
Corrupting the minds!

Life then was simple,
Clear as straight line
And Mother Nature
Was not yet being raped
By mountains of concrete,
Steel and decorated by
Colorful Neon lights!

Love and peace
Magically blended
In the hearts of mankind:
Hatred, greed and envy
Were never in existence!

No rush, worries or stress
But a simple life
Fully enjoyed to the fullest,
Loving and caring for each other
While embedded with respect
Was then the ultimate goal!

BARBARA SUEN

Barbara Suen is from Mishawaka, Indiana. She is 52. An age of wonder! Wondering where the "time" went after the busyness of raising three children and working. She enjoys writing prose poetry, and has been published in "Soul Fountain" and "The Storyteller" magazines. She has also been published in several poetry anthologies, of which she is very proud of. Her dream is to publish her own book of poetry! Like she tells her children, even now, "it all starts with a vision"!

Be Still And Know

By: Author Barbara Suen

Feeling numb on the outside,
emotions hidden
yet, a restlessness churns inside
like a tiger in a cage
pacing
back and forth
back and forth
until exhaustion sets in

I am this.
In my own cage
no plans for the day,
and if there were,
they would go unfinished...
visits cut short
they say
I have one foot out the door
when I get there.

What is the hurry?
What are these worries?
That are so powerful
it keeps me on the edge
of the ledge of existence
Frozen
fully engaged ?
no.
What
Keeps me caged
enraged?

Peace? I cried,
on this bright, August morning
It came to me...
I had not prayed for a long time.
maybe he is waiting
to hear from me,
like a father would wait for his daughter to call.

"Our father who art in heaven"
can you hear me?
It's me... "Barbara"
"I've been away too long,
I know."

BARBARA SUEN

Barbara Suen is from Mishawaka, Indiana. She is 52. An age of wonder! Wondering where the "time" went after the busyness of raising three children and working. She enjoys writing prose poetry, and has been published in "Soul Fountain" and "The Storyteller" magazines. She has also been published in several poetry anthologies, of which she is very proud of. Her dream is to publish her own book of poetry! Like she tells her children, even now, "it all starts with a vision"!

Behind The Stained Glass

By: Author Barbara Suen

Where is heaven?
Where is hell?
Up there, or down there?
Are we there already?
Hell?
Some say it is so.
Is it a point system?
"Stars" for your acts of goodwill.
Sitting behind the stained glass,
trying to soak it all in...
A beautiful place.
But, no one was smiling,
I swear.

Heaven and Hell
or nothing at all.

I had a taste of both.
Heaven surrounded me,
with love and warmth
But, only when I had no expectations.
Easy to remember.
"Happy" is just so easy to remember.
I just couldn't hold on to it.

Hell.
Loses everything.
Don't get too close to the fire
It's greedy. Want's all of you.
I expected Love, as if I deserved it.
Unconditional, from all.
I had expectations....more and more.
Lost it all.

Burnt and blistered heart.
I am there in gray, standing with the unforgiven and forgotten.
Trumpets above, screams below.
I look up when I pray.
I look up.

Beg, Borrow Renee', Just Don't Steal

By: Author/Mom Renee' Drummond-Brown

It was as though it was yesterday;
you were only four years old.
Off to Greater Works Christian Academy;
on the school bus in the cold.

On your first day of school,
I stood there with you anticipating the nervous wait.
Little did we both know;
you'd later be that scholar student athlete, with
straight A's.

As only
'YOU AND I' stood there; you held onto my leg
with such fright. While I,
was 'ALWAYS' holding onto God for the both of us;
EV'R
'SO' VERY TIGHT!

You later became an academic scholar.
Proving to me, to be, all you could be.
MVP; Tri County Christian league,
Basketball Player of the year, and YES
School MVP!

GWA closed its door in your tenth grade year. 'BUT GOD',
sends a ram in a bush, and
Mount Alvernia Catholic High School appears!

You also, put that school
on the map. Setting records.
Winning WPIAL,
and placing at state.
Not to mention, MVP,
graduating with Honors, full scholarship offers, running all over
God's plate!

You did not select the colleges
too big nor too far. So, you chose
Edinboro University, and there too; you were God's stand out
star!

You immediately earned the title;
"Freshman of Western Pennsylvania" my dear.
Capturing championship after championship,
trips, awards, rings, and
Edinboro's senior Nancy Acker Women's Athlete of the year!

You had Edinboro University ranked #2 in the Nation. Again
you're recognized a scholar student athlete, records set,
MVP, and all before your first college graduation!

We marched on;
GOD, YOU, and I, with
an Academic Scholarship into the Master's program.
And when times got very hard, we both cried and 'held on' tighter to
'THE'
I AM THAT I AM!

On May 10, 2014,
Congratulations were in order on your
Master's degree in Educational Leadership.
My God.
And at only 23 years of age. What
an accomplishment!!!

West Virginia University Doctoral Program,
here we (GOD, dad, mom, and Renee') come!
God, You said in Your word that You
would never leave nor forsake us.
So, we thank You in advance
for NEVER, EVER leaving 'us' alone!

Renee', you dare ask me the question;
"If, I get accepted mom; how can we afford this?" My child,
"God has already shown me your favorable decision for WVU;
if you will. Renee', we'll simply beg, borrow; we just won't steal!"

Dedicated to:

Riding on the shoulders of giants!

CONGRATULATIONS

DR. RENEE' BARBARA-ANN BROWN,

WEST VIRGINIA UNIVERSITY, CLASS OF 2017!

My soul looks back and wonders Renee'...how did we make it over (Mommy)?

A B.A.D. Poem

BLACK 'LIES' MATTER TOO!

By: Author Renee' Drummond-Brown

Compulsive liar
Habitual too!
White lies,
little lies;
black lies matter too!
Truth be told,

she 'NEVER'
swore
to tell the truth;
the whole truth,
an'
'nothin'
BUT
the truth.
So, help her Satan.
Fabrication.
Yeah,
let it
do
what it do!

Dedicated to: *PINOCCHIO THEORY*

A B.A.D. Poem

NANCY NDEKE

Name:
Nancy Ndeke
Nationality:
Kenyan.
Residence:
Nairobi.
Career:
Teacher for two decade's
Consultant on conflict management with Multimedia consultant (Nairobi).
OTHERS
Child protection services.
Gender equality's sensitization activities.
Theater and drama artist
Author
Poet
And mother.

BLOOD DOES NOT SHUT UP

By: Author Nancy Ndeke

Blood doesn't shut up
Or sleep easy on
The road
The sand
The bush
The valley
The dungeon
The dark forest
The unmarked grave
The highest mountain
It cries
For it's kin
It's own
It howls
Rumbles for
Justice of innocent
In loud ruckus
For the dog under
It weeps
For the unborn
It gnashes it's teeth
For the old unable to flee war
It curses
It run's wild abroad

Calling the church bell
To dare see
The rains of death
The forced still births
The oceans of abortion
The cry blinden
It deafens
Till slumber waken
Ignorance barks
The Lords of gods
Must look again
Consult without insult
Confirm the results
Of the entrails
That had informed
The hand that had shed blood
For the flood cries
And won't stop
Till the actors of the Acts
Whose anthem is solid fear
Selling for free in our street's
Oooh how BLOOD CRIES!!!!!!
For it's own.

Blood Stained Banner

By: Author Renee' Drummond-Brown

As I pierce
the deep
blue skies
returning home
questioning
'not'
who?
What?
When?
Where?
Nor
why?
Shoeless
'BUT'
got His
favorite
BLOOD STAINED DRESS ON!

Some say it ain't so
but,
if 'He'
can walk on water
to me,
then
through
mustard seed
faith

an'
'sum'
belief;
I too
can
gaze
across
the shore,
calm
the raging seas,
keeping
mine eyes
fixed
only
on Him;
all the more.
And 'YES'
drown
into
ETERNITY.

Dedicated to:
At a 'TREE', at a tree (Acts 5:30); is where I first saw the light
and the burdens of my heart were rolled away.
Yeah,
that's where it 'twas'~~~I received my sight!!!

A B.A.D. Poem

Boisterous Rains

By: Author Renee' Drummond-Brown

They
don't
perfess
to know
'ev'rythang.'
But…
they do
know…
gutsy
storm clouds
rise.
They do know
bout
'sum'
rainy 'dayze!'
They've 'ev'n' heard
the song writer
'sang'
"strong winds 'DO' blow."
They know(s)
bout
them 'ragin' seas
tossing 'em'
to N' fro.

I don't perfess
to know
many 'thangs'
but what
I do know;
like them,
I too,
squally
in tempestuous
Boisterous
Rains.

Dedicated to: *My sistah-Denise Boozer and son, Retired NFL Player, Leander Jordan*

A B.A.D. Poem

Can I Have 'Sum'?

By: Author Renee' Drummond-Brown

Root Beer and Moon pies hide.
Its obvious, chocolate on the outside.
Swing low, sweet 'shugga' 'iz' within
Mommy 'SNEAKS' rattling paper at night.
But I hear her; I'm listening!
Can I have 'sum'; 'outta' sight?
Can't have 'NOTHIN' to 'MY' 'SELF'!!!
Mommy waited all day for night.
Here I come; disappointing, her bite.

Dedicated to: *Root Beer and Moon Pies go together minus the 'kidz'!!!*

A B.A.D. Poem

Can't We All Just Get Along? Hell Naw!

By: Author Renee' Drummond-Brown

Rodney King
asked
"Can't we
all
just get along?"
I say…
HELL
to the
naw!

UNLESS,
'WE' 'WRITE'
'ALL'
wrongs!
Raped,
hung,
burned,
beaten,
scorned,
shot
and yes
'ev'n'
pic'NIG' torched;
while
'YOU'
spectators
watched!

"Can't we
'all'
just get along?"
Hell
to the
naw!
UNLESS,
you
give 'ME'

'MY'
40 acres
'ANNA'
mule
and only
then...
I'll be gone.

Other
than that.
I say,
HELL
to the
naw!

Dedicated to: *HELL to the naw.*

A B.A.D. Poem

Citation

By: Author Renee' Drummond-Brown

I'll write a poem for you;
You write a poem for me.
Back to back; quotations extract 'summadat'
'BUT' remember to cite thee; PLEASE.
Illustrations' mention references; citation is key.
I'll write a poem for you;
You write a poem for me.
Son of citation will allow thee,
to be or not to be;
"A BAD Poem" if you please.

Dedicated to:

Drummond-Brown, R. (2017). A B.A.D. Poem. Bloomington, IN: AuthorHouse.

A B.A.D. Poem

CLARESE RENEE WHITE

By: Author Renee' Drummond-Brown

"Whosover therefore
shall humble himself
as this
little child,
the same is greatest in the kingdom of heaven"
(Matthew 18:4 KJV.)
Clarese Renee White,
God designed
'THAT' Scripture,
no doubt.
Not to boast;
but,
with 'YOU' my child,
in mind.
Signed,
THE FATHER,
SON
and
HOLY GHOST.

Letitia gave birth
to an angel,
on 2-23-94,
in Clarksville Tennessee;
Blachfield Army Medical Hospital
is where
*'OUR' **Clarese***
was born.
BUT GOD,

does the unthinkable,
an' chose
t'HIS' beautiful blackbird; (like the Raven),
to exit her earthly Ark, stage right,
an' 'YES'
soar;
'ev'r' so high
with His divine wings on…
mid-flight,
into
the heavenly skies!

She's free of pain,
free of personal gain.
Yeah,
'OUR' angel **Clarese,**
NOW ROAMS
to an' fro;
as of July, Twentieth,
Two thousand and Seventeen,
12:30 midnight
to be
exact.
She's free of sin,
throughout
the firmaments.
She made it.
She made it in,
holding

onto the hem,
of His
garment.

Clarence and Sharon
you were Clarese's right arm.
Now
the hour has come
for you both
to carry on;
her prophetic gift
of love
without
any regret(s).
When times get hard
and I assure you
'THEY WILL'.
Just remember her marks' set,
her marks' left
of purity,
which will
continuously
hold us
onto
her precious, precious, 'PRECIOUS' memories yet.

For a time, such as this,
we must draw from her

inner strength,
when need be;
as we attempt
to sojourn on
without
her physical body
present.

Clarese
is already missed.
Sealed with 'our' kiss
of lasting memories…
by all of her friends
and family.
Especially from,
Uncle Kendal, Aunt Sanese
and cousin
little Miss Kendal.
But mainly
by none other,
than her (only) loving brother
Darrius.

She so adored
family
who
could do her
no wrong.

Again, I say,
She's
loved,
loved,
loved,
by Mom
Letitia,
Brother Darrius,
Pap-Pap, Clarence,
Grandma Sharon and adopted Grammy
BAD,
Uncle Kendal,
Little Miss Kendal,
and lest we forget
her very 'own'
Auntie,
AKA,
big sis,
Sanese.

Clarese

so, so, so, loved
John S. Charlton school,
lounging,
traveling,
bowling,
coloring with green crayola's
AND UNQUESTIONABLY
had no problem making you

go buy
her
some popsicles too!
Any 'colour'
for her,
would ABSOLUTELY do (smile-LOL)!
Did I mention
green was her color
of the day;
equated to Jesus,
nothing
but His rich earth
would have
her last say.

Clarese *loved us*
'ALL'
unconditionally;
like Christ
loved
His Only
Begotten Son.
She too
gave family 'ALL'
she had to give
and expected
nothing
in return;
but
sheer love

66

from each and every-one
(of them).

She lived a life
of purpose
and meaning.
Clarese *taught us*
(at least me)
some learned lessons
in which, we ought to live
just
to make it in,
into
His Kingdom;
that will
enviably come.
We too,
like her
must live
a life of humility,
blameless, guiltless
simplistic
and ever so free….

Clarese,
wasn't afraid
to fuss,
getting things
off her chest.

NOPE;
she held nothing back,
you see,
feisty, fierce,
and 'HONEST'
as can be.
That trait
will truly
be missed,
by
the White family.

Now family an' friends,
rejoice, dance and sing,
Clarese *is at*
a Holy Ghost party
with
'The Father'
wearing her 'green'
designer wings!
Hair on Fleek,
nails done.
and no more
autistic memories.
NO
NADDA ONE!

Our baby fought,
a good fight

from beginning to end;
but knew
where
to cast her cares.
YES,
she stared Autism
right
in the eye
an' 'NEVER' gave up
nor
gave in!!!
She 'WAITED'
on God to move,
an' say,
"job well done my faithful devoted servant;
Now **Clarese,**
you come on home
and rest
in 'MY' Ark
with popsicle streets
paved
in pure gold."

CLARESE RENEE WHITE
"Whosoever shall receive one of such children in my name,
receiveth me:
and
whosoever shall receive me,
receiveth not me,

but
him that sent me" (Mark 9:37 KJV.)
*May you **Clarese,***
with 'Y'OUR' Father,
who art in Heaven,
FINALLY
GET SOME MUCH-NEEDED
and
DESERVED 'REST';
IN HIS
PEACE!

Dedicated to: *The White family*
In Memory of: *CLARESE RENEE WHITE*

From: *The Drummond and Brown Family.*
We are truly sorry for your loss and we love you.

CLARESE RENEE WHITE

(Sunrise 2-23-1994-Sunset 7-20-2017)

By: Author Renee' Drummond-Brown

C aring
L oving
A dored
R ighteous
E asy
S aved
E cclesiastical

R eal
E nthusiastic
N ice
E vangelical
E nergetic

W itness
H oly
I ntense
T ruth
E ternal

Dedicated to: *Clarence and Sharon White*
In Memory of: *'THEIR ANGEL' LITTLE MISS CLARESE RENEE WHITE*

From: *The Drummond and Brown Family.*
We are truly sorry for your loss and we love you.

CONVICTION

By: Author Renee' Drummond-Brown

In my
poetic
text,
I judiciously
script
religion
money
politics
and/or
sex.

Therefore,
one
should
'NEVA'
take
my poetic scribes
out of
context.

Dedicated to: *The verdict is in.*

A B.A.D. Poem

BLANCA ALICIA GARZA

Blanca Alicia Garza is a Poet from Las Vegas, Nevada. She is a nature and animal lover, and enjoys spending time writing. Her poems are published in the Poetry Anthologies, "Moonlight Dreamers of Yellow Haze", and "Dandelions in a Vase of Roses" now available at Amazon.com. Blanca's work can be found in The Poet Community, Whispers, The Winamop Journal, Indiana Voice Journal, Tuck Magazine, Raven's Cage Ezine, Scarlet Leaf Review as well as Birdsong Anthology 2016, Vol 1.

Crimson Faith

By: Author Blanca Alicia Garza

Losing my faith
In all of humanity
Shedding of blood
Sowing of hatred
between races
Creating barriers
instead of bonds
for a better world
Things are valued
People devalued
Our blood is all
crimson in color
our beautiful skin
of many shades
We need to spread
seeds of kindness
not more of hate.
Joining forces,
building bridges
instead of walls
We are together
in this world
We are destroying it
by beliefs and hatred
Enough fallen Angel's
without any fault
Stop the hate and
spread peace and love.

Cycles

By: Author Renee' Drummond-Brown

Momma told her not to do IT.
IT was done; she did not LISTEN
LISTEN to her, for what, and why, she too did it, AFTER-ALL?
AFTER-ALL, she had her at 16.
16, she, herself, should've been pristine CLEAN.
CLEAN as bleach on a summers CLOTHESLINE.
CLOTHESLINES, yeah, not soils hung out to DRY.
DRY stains. Tide can't even get these out, nor CAN;
CAN a praise and/or SHOUT!
SHOUT it out!!! Should've been playin wit dolls, jacks and balls til 9:00.
NINE months to GO.
GO to jail…do not pass go til 18
EIGHTEEN-year BIDS.
BIDS her FAREWELL.
FAREWELL Momma says, "I told you so."

Dedicated to: Recurrences

DARK SHADOWS

By: Author Renee' Drummond-Brown

Shadows
come an'
be gone.

Shadows
will
leave you
to fend
in the sun.
All alone.

Shadows come
as they grow.
An' wait
for no one.
This
I do know.

Dedicated to: Throwing Shade.

"DATS' 'MY' 'COUZIN"

By: Author Renee' Drummond-Brown

Some will say
"OH'
that Renee'.
she writes
'JUST'
OK."

Some will say,
"She got
a lil'
'sumthin; 'sumthin'
to say.
I guess,
its
OK"
???

Some will say
"it's alright
the way
she writes.
BUT….
then again

I've seen
MUCH BETTER
INK PENS."

Some will say
"I like
the way she thinks…
'BUT'…
So, and so
has a
'MUCH'
BETTER FLOW
to his
and/or
her
ink."

But Maya,
when I
ARRIVE.
'ALL'
will say
"I
BEEN
KNOWING
'THAT'
RENEE'
'FROM'
WaaaaaaaaaaaaaaaaaaaaaaaY

79

back
in the day.
She's a prolific writer
with a lot
to say
from
within."

'FUNNY',
I too,
knew
Dr. Maya Angelou,
from
back then.
She's my
'TWICE REMOVED'
cousin's cousin.

Dedicated to: *I been 'knowin' her.*

A B.A.D. Poem

Dear Chinua Achebe

Author – Ngozi Olivia Osuoha

At night, in the village square
At gathering for moonlight tales
I tell the dwindling hope of my people,
In a theatre it unfolds like a movie
I see their agony,
In a theatre like a sugeon stitching a torn flesh,
I feel their pain
I watch them wail and weep
As they swim in aches and navigate the trauma,
Penetrate the pores of hardship
And permeate the rocks of starvation
Because the center holds no more
Things are falling apart
And they are no longer at ease,
They mourn like a widow mourning her murdered son
And a virgin weeping for her slain soldier.

From the river bank i watch
As the storm disband fishes
And wave blow up beaches
I watch tide sweep the shores away.

Titanic, yet sinking
Rowing, yet steady
Floating, yet drowning
Coagulating debris and fungi
Dead, like a dead sea.

Far from the madding crowd
I watch the struggle
As they labour and toil in vain
Harvesting vanity and waste
The outrageous disaster,
And the flooding blood
A rhetorical question
None dares ask nor answer.

Dear Chinua Achebe
Things are falling apart
I think there was a country with the arrow of God
Maybe they kept it like those that captured "the ark of covenant."

The banner of illiteracy engulfed our land
And chain of ignorance betrothed our fate,
The fetters of superstition clouded our peace
Then came the egocentric god to rescue
The god that indeed came against us, used us against us
The stranger that bought our ancestors
Enslaved our fathers, married our mothers
The tyrant that we served, guarded and worshipped
That one, that broke our center
Cracked our wall and made us fall apart
The one that sold and bought us for nothing.

Dear Chinua Achebe,
He bewitched us to practise witchcraft on ourselves
Till now things remain fallen apart
As though our womb bore no talents
As if our land was thorn instead of crown
As though we had no patriarch of gold
Brave and bold,
As if there was no matriarch of ruby, sacred and consecrated.

dear god

By: Author Renee' Drummond-Brown

dear god,
why'd alice
pen
my song?
the color
use to be
dr. maya angelou.
now,
its 'jus'
purple.

Yeah,
it'll do;
'jus' fine.
celies'
a lil'
seasoned
'wit'
'summa-me'
an'
'summadat'
shugs
mess.
you guessed;
'ov'r'
a lifetime
of
peculiarity
an'
(like her)
no-one
understanding
me
being shy.
a lifetime
'makin'
sure
'evr'yone's'
happy
an'
cares-less
bout

how i feel(s)
inside.

dear god,
why don't
they
understand me
or
the colors
i brang.
why don't they
understand
that
i'm loyal
throughout
eternity.
why don't they
know…
i'm purple…
yeah,
'dat' be me~~~
mrs.
royalty.

'naw',
'jus' 'kiddin'
though,
that ain't
hardly
me
at all.

cause
the color purple
is
so
very vain
you see;
an' yes
alice walker,
you probably
penned
'dat' book
bout
me.

alice,
i ain't
hardly
purple.
i'm
'jus'
dr.
maya angelou's
prodigy.

Dedicated to: *your so vain; i bet you wrote the book bout me.*

A B.A.D. Poem

Dear John,

By: Author Renee' Drummond-Brown

DRUMMOND

Dear John,
I hope
this poem
finds you
in the best of health.
I love you
BUT...
I found
someone else.

He's actually
your best friend
and
my babies'
dad.
I promise you though,
he
did-not
destroy
what you and I
once had.

I just grew tired
of you
being away
so
very long.
One thing led
to another;
felt so right
an' yet
so wrong.
We tried to tell you
before
you left
for war.
But then
like the Temptations
we both thought
another
mind war;
hmm~~~
what is it good for?

So,
as stated before,
I love you,
BUT…
I found someone else~~~
that I
just
absolutely
adore.

Dear Jody,
Oh,
no one
must've
told you,
an' you still
don't know?
I married
your
best friend
LONG; LONG
LOOOOONG
before
I left home.

She gets
'YOUR'
allotments,
medical coverage,
social security
and
my pension too.
We're on an island
(military base)
'laughin'
our butts off;
bout
how
WE BOTH
PLAYED YOU!

Hey Jody,
How's them projects;
I left you in?
All them mixed babies?
The welfare checks
and my drug dealing
best friend?

Sorry sister girl,
you got played in the end.
See you,
when we come home
with
our
son,
daughter,
dog
and
Mercedes Benz.
Love John,
Your ex-lover and best friend.

Dedicated to: Oorah~~~Semper Fidelis~~~You 'gotta'
pay to play 'wit' a few good men!!!

A B.A.D. Poem

Death Becomes Her

By: Author Renee' Drummond-Brown

*I saw
death
today.
Stared her
right
in the face;
and said
"No!
Not now!
Not on today!"
She callously
moved
'outta'
my way;
went
onto another
soul mate
an' had
her way.
Well,
tomorrows
another
un-promised
date.*

Dedicated to: *No man knows 'His' hour; get ready for your death date.*

A B.A.D. Poem

Demon

By: Author Renee' Drummond-Brown

It's 'NOT'
your child.
It's the narcotics
within
he and/or she
running wild!

But…
The Father says
Love on 'em';
NOT THE DEMON
'ANYHOW'!

They 'wanna'
change.
They 'wanna'
chance.
They 'wanna'
'SANG';
a song
to a different
dance.

GET BEHIND THEM SATAN!!!
GOD,
I'M 'BEGGIN' YOU…
GIVE 'EM'
A SECOND CHANCE!!!

Dedicated to: *Satan; flee!!!* God give 'em' peace within~~~Peace be still.

A B.A.D. Poem

Disgust

By: Author Renee' Drummond-Brown

I loathe
that big bed,
cause
more slaves
are
made!

I detest Massa
an'
'WISH'
he was
'DEAD';
instead!

I despise
Missy;
she pretend
she don't
'SEE'!

I dislike
her kids
who 'LOVE'
'MY'
chocolate breast
and
suckling
'BEST'!

I 'HATE'
my 'OWN' kids
cause
they
belong
to him
and
not
me!

Dedicated to: *Genetic connection!*

A B.A.D. Poem

Do You Have The Time?

By: Author Renee' Drummond-Brown

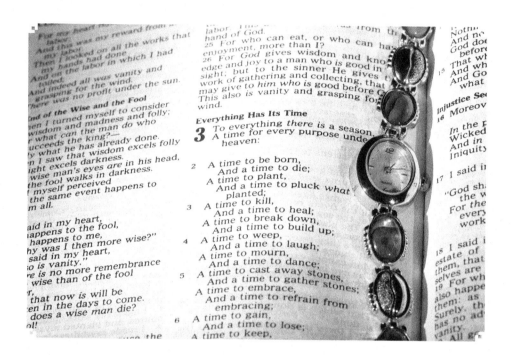

I listen
to the
tic
in the
heart
of
the clock;
as it
tocs.

I
'WATCH'
the face
of
the clock
'TELL TIME'
of
tale-tell signs
as death
passes by;
like
an ancient
fob watch,
telling
those
never-ending
lies
about
time
passing
her
'bye'.

Dedicated to: No man knows the hour; 'NO'.... Not one.

A B.A.D. Poem

DON'T 'NOBODY' 'BRANG' me "NO. BAD NEWS!!!"

By: Author Renee' Drummond-Brown

At 52.
Naw….
I'm 'lyin';
'jus'
'kiddin' me
'sum' you.

At the best
time
in my life.
So,
don't
"NOBODY"
brang me
'Nadda'
misery;
nor
a
strife.
Cause
my size 9's.
Well…
I'll leave that
up to
the mind.
Of you
???

DON'T 'NOBODY'
'BRANG' me
"NO. BAD NEWS!!!"
Cause,
my arms
is
too short
to box
'wit' God.
BUT...
my feet(s)
'N'
shoes;
WELL~~~
we'll walk
all 'ov'r'
you.
DON'T 'NOBODY'
'BRANG' me
"NO. BAD NEWS!!!"

Let's 'jus'
say
for the sake
of 'sayin'
they'll
definitely
do
what they do
('kickin' 'sum' WHAT?)
an'
I AIN'T
PLAYIN'!!!
DON'T 'NOBODY'
'BRANG' me
"NO. BAD NEWS!!!"
SHUT-UP.
Renee' Drummond-Brown.

Dedicated to: *All God's 'chillins' got 'sum' shoes and my size 9's; do what it do!!!*

A B.A.D. Poem

Double Dutch Bus

By: Author Renee' Drummond-Brown

Shoop
de'
Shoop.
'Dis'
ain't no
hula-hoop.
It's 'dat'
double dutch
rope.
'Dat' do
what
it do.
'Talkin'
'bout'
'da'
loop de' loop.
Shoop.
Shoop.

Yeah,
'IZ' shook it
to
'da' east.
'IZ' shook it
to
'da' west.

I shook my butt off
on 'dat'
double dutch
bus!

Shoop
de'
Shoop.
'Dis'
ain't no
hula-hoop.
It's 'dat'
double dutch
rope.
'Dat' do
what
it do.
'Talkin'
'bout'
'da'
loop de' loop.
Shoop.
Shoop.

Nappy!
Bald as can be;
aint' stopped
'dis'
big bone neck,

ashey black legs
an
brown
crusted feets'
from doing
the
'dawg'
on 'thang'.
Shoop
de'
shoop.
'Dis'
ain't no
hula-hoop.
It's the
double dutch
rope.
'Dat' do
what
it do.
'Talkin'
'bout'
'da'
loop de' loop.
Shoop.
Shoop.

Yeah
i
rolls my eyes

and
stomps'
'myze'
feets,
cause in
'DAT'
rope
'dis' dark sustah's
confidant
'AZ'
can be.

Shoop
de'
shoop.
'Dis'
ain't no
hula-hoop.
It's 'dat'
double dutch
rope.
'Dat' do
what
it do.
'Talkin'
'bout'
'da'
loop de' loop.
Shoop.
Shoop.

Shoop.
Shoop.

Shoop.
Shoop.

Shoop.
Shoop.
'Dis'
ain't no
hula-hoop.
Its 'dat'
double dutch bus
that
do
what it do.

Dedicated to: *1, 2, 3, 4; get ready, jump in, an' 'ev'n' 'dat' score. Shoop de' shoop!!!*

A B.A.D. Poem

DREAM(s)

Weaved Collaboration Poem By:
Authors/Sisters Nancy Ndeke (Kenya Nairobi)
and Renee Drummond-Brown(Pittsburgh, Pennsylvania)

Nancy Ndeke (Kenya Nairobi)
DREAM(s)
Dare to
Come true
Not if…but
When pursued
Not
With vigor
Not
Relentlessly
But
Forcefully
Like a thief in the night;
even Upon a morn,
but 12:00 noon is the best time for dreams to shed our poetic vision(s) ever so bright.

Dedicated to: *'WE' have a poetic dream; like a King.*

Ease On Down the Road

By: Author Renee' Drummond-Brown

How did we
'ov'r-come?
Our soul
looks back an' wonders;
'JUST'
what type
of dirt
we're made of?

Like a lion
to its den.
Like a tin man
to its oil.
Like a scarecrow
to its straw;
down the road
we eased.
We ease on down the road;
lest we fall.

Dedicated to: *Don't you carry 'nothin'.*

A B.A.D. Poem

Ebony 'N' Ivory

By: Author Renee' Drummond-Brown

Adam is
black
as the night.
Eve is
white
as the snow.
Her forbidden
fruit
bruises
the heel;
garden eviction
is
Adams
unlawful plight.
History made known
this
'fo' 'sho';
Eve's children
belong
to
blackest nights.
Oldest fossils found
are Lucy's;
right?

Dedicated to: In the beginning; God created the end.

A B.A.D. Poem

Susan Joyner-Stumpf is originally from New Orleans and now calls the Colorado Rockies her home with her husband and menagerie of animal friends. She has been writing since the age of seven. It started off as an escape mechanism for Susan, for she was suffering from Childhood Abuse. After a while, it became a passion, and after 37 published books and still counting, and appearing in over 20 United States AND International Anthologies, the rest is history.

Susan started her own Publishing Company two and a half years ago called WILDFIRE PUBLICATIONS, having made her best friend, Deborah Brooks Langford, as Vice-President and Marketing Director. Together, Deb and Susan are also starting up their own Live Blog Radio Show on Red River Radio Station called RHYTHM AND MUSE INTERVIEWS. Also, they've extended the services of WILDFIRE PUBLICATIONS to include a monthly magazine entitled WILDFIRE PUBLICATIONS MONTHLY MAGAZINE, which is doing quite well.

Susan feels that her writing career, spanning over MORE than half her life span thus far, has been a life-long journey of pleasure and pain into that great Unknown. She writes to help herself as well as to help others heal. It is Susan's humble objective to keep the Arts alive as well as to help her readers find oneness in a driven, stressful world strewn with bits and pieces.

ELEMENT OF SKY

By: Author ♥ Susan Joyner–Stumpf

1.

When the overhead
      Is beyond our

                    Timid imaginations

And touch
Too real of latent
      Dream to rise
From reluctant birth ~ ~

      We must peer inside The unfathomableness
         Of ourselves . . .

Tiny integers in the swirling
      Soft glimmer of vacuumed space

Alas drag the wounded fears from
      Their swollen pools,

   Believe that we are as real
As the passions that
      Define us,

The catalysts that
Embellish life forms of their own
        From singular, lonely vision
Resting inert beneath
        Self-conscious tunnels Of undulation.

2.

A place and time when Silence was safer
        Action more centered In its framework of minimal tears.

        We're only as close to Stars
As what brightness we
        Allow to drape Our hidden darknessnes,
        Silhouette forms milky monograms
Of grayscale remnants
        Of everything we ever tried to be but didn't
            And all we tried to feel

                      And yet were left empty Instead.

3.

How harmony is
        Corralled

Or connections sealed
        Is not merely the blend and scope
        Of what once lay screaming, unearthed,

But how we finally step outside of cosmic boundaries,

The gulf of what we perceived

As limitations....

And realize

~ ~ Oh and realize . . .

That deep within the crevasses of
Us all,

Therein lies an infinite

And waiting

Element of

Sky.

Facade

By: Author Renee' Drummond-Brown

We laugh
cuddle
an'
hug.
We live
to
make love~~~
Then
the
name calls
hurt;
we cut,
tear down
each other's
worth.
Then
we laugh
cuddle
an'
hug.
We live
to make love~~~
Then
the
name calls
hurt;
we cut,

tear down
each other's
worth.
Then
we laugh
cuddle
an'
hug.
We live
to make love~~~
IT'S
ALL
A
FAÇADE.
Cause
love
don't
love us
at all!!!

Dedicated to: *Your move.*

A B.A.D. Poem

Fiddler on the Roof

By: Author Renee' Drummond-Brown

He,
plants the seed.
Momma, tills
them ground(s).
Sacrificial womb
unappreciated frowns.
Lamb
amongst wolves,
tread
un-earthly bound.
Pulled
from our yoke
consumed;
where there's fire
'THERE IS SMOKE'.

Dusk before dark,
morning fore noon,
night before day,
gone
way too soon.

'IF'
we must die;
let it be
alone.
No fiddlers
on the roof,
need play
for me,
'dem'
sad
sad
songs.

Party 'ov'r' here
as I
transition home!

Dedicated to: *Rejoice at death; cry at birth!*

A B.A.D. poem

Krista puts emotions from life experiences, into written words. Her poetry is a personal form of expression. She strives to encourage and give hope to the reader. Krista is the 2016 Realistic Poetry International Contest winner. In her free time she mentors up and coming young poets and is an avid volunteer for many causes in her community, where she resides in Virginia Beach, Virginia. Her work has been published in numerous literary publications all over the world.

FIFTY YEARS OF GLORY

(Brown vs Board of Education)

By: Author Krista Vowell Clark

Topeka, Kansas, May 17, 1954.
A historic day, that opened many, a door.

Black brothers and sisters, struck down segregation.
It was time to make the USA, a glorious nation.

President Eisenhower agreed to join the case.
He, too, wanted us to love our neighbor, regardless of race.

Oliver Brown's daughter, Linda, traveled far, to "All Black ", Monroe School.
Forced to pass by white children, saying things that were cruel!

Whites turned the 14th amendment into their own interpretation.
While blacks took a stand, against racial segregation.

Chief Justice, Thurgood Marshall, fought for Civil Rights.
He helped open doors, and turn on lights.

This historic day, makes me feel happy, yet numb.
Although a victory, the fight had just begun.

First and Last

By: Author Renee' Drummond-Brown

R
EN
EE'D
RUMM
OND-BR
OWN
NAME.

Dedicated to: *You don't know my name.*

Fools Rush In!

By: Author Renee' Drummond-Brown

Elvis
once sang
"wise men say,
'ONLY'
fools rush in."
He ain't
'nevalied'
'bout'
'US'
simple women.

We meet 'em' on today;
tomorrow
they're
moved in.

We care
'NOTHIN'
bout
our children's
'feelins'.

He takes 'ov'r'
the house
an'
gets served
like a king.
While
our babies
'gotta'
tip-toe
round
$hhhhhhhhhhhh
quiet,
as a
church-mouse.
~~~~~
IN
THEIR OWN HOUSE!!!

It's 'jus'
emotions
that take
'US'
'ov'r'
cause he
gets
the best
of our
'luv';
more or less.

But Kenny sang;
'YOU'
'gotta'
'KNOW'
when
to
hold him.
When
to fold him.
And 'yezzz',
'EVEN'
when
to run!

Frankie Lymon,
why do fools
rush in?
When you gave
'US'
the
A B C's
of
'luv'

Dedicated to: *She's jus' a 'FOOL' in 'luv' 'wit' you.*

A B.A.D. Poem

FOR THOSE

By: Author Renee' Drummond-Brown

*For those
who pushed
us
in
the back
of*

them
rooms,
an'
kept
'tellin' us
we were slow.
But God
and
'dem'
black mommas
said
"it ain't so,"
an'
said
'YES'
to their
every no.

For those
who
put us down
an'
made us
eat
'sum' crow.
But God
and
'dem'
black mommas
said

127

"it ain't so;"
an'
'YES'
to their
every no.

For those
who
didn't believe
in us
going
off
to college,
to an' fro.
But God
and
'dem'
black mommas
said
"it ain't so;"
an'
'YES'
to their
every no.

For those
who
refuse
to listen

to
what truth,
we now
know.
But God
and
'dem'
black mommas
said
"it ain't so;"
an'
'YES'
to their
every no.

For those
who
held us back
an'
stunted
our
'very'
'own'
growth.
But God
and
'dem'
black mommas
said
"it ain't so;"

an'
'YES'
to their
every no.

FOR THOSE
THAT
DID NOT
KNOW...

'HE'
PROMISED US:
THE LAST
WOULD FINISH
FIRST.

JUST
IN CASE

'YOU'

~~~

DIDN'T
KNOW!

Dedicated to: *'THOSE' Brilliant Momma's.*

A B.A.D. Poem

ANNETTE NASSER

Annette Nasser lives comfortably in Fall River, MA. An avid food photographer and writer, she has been published in Literary House Review, A Hudson View Poetry Digest, Spinnings, Apple Fruits of the Old Oak as well as various literary magazines, journals and anthologies and has received a past award for Celebrated Thoughts.

FOR YOU

By: Author Annette Nasser

Author's Note: *The following poem I originally wrote in honor of a writer and fellow friend, who, at the time, had been cared for by Hospice. Shortly after I wrote this poem, he passed away. My poem is dedicated to all who suffer in illness, terminal or otherwise, and for those who are the caregivers, for they too, feel for the person who is ill.*

We see life and death in every moment,
Every flicker of light, we walk through
Every dream, every prayer, every day, every night
We grow in every instance, with every living,
Dying cell, in illness, in being well.
We breathe essence given by family, friends,
By what is perceived, what is felt, from beginning to end
We give, we live to love, we pray
For those who choose to stay, or go.
We pray with strength to stand, firm, strong,
Aid the weak, help them see our love to assist,
To honor, fulfill their need to be comforted
Life shifts, motivates, moves in light,

The flame, spark, fading flicker moves in dark,
Nesting into what may seem silence,
Stillness, endless dreams
Power, wisdom, we walk within
Circle of existence, harmony with earth,
With affection, reflection, breathing life, breathing words
Of love and grace, of tender care for whose breath
Needs to feel, be comforted for strength, minute, hour,
Day or night passing by
We see, we walk,
We grow we give, we breathe, we live to give
To love to pray gently, every night, every day,
For you.

JACK KOLKMEYER

Jack holds a B.A. in English Literature/Creative Writing from Ohio University and an M.P.A. in Public Affairs/Urban and Regional Planning from the School of Public and Environmental Affairs at Indiana University.

Jack resides and writes in Delray Beach, Florida. His current writing projects include poetry, music and city planning topics and several screenplays.

*He recently completed **Higher Glyphics,** his first, full-length book of poetry.*

gaining perspective

By: Author Jack Kolkmeyer

it may feel backward
the more forward we go
watching those blurred images swirling
*   between then and now*
whisking off into there

that we all see things differently
*   even though we see the same things*

there are reasons for this
*   although reasoning has little to do with it*

it is more about imaging
*   and imagining what is there*
*   or not there*
*   or might be there*

it is only when we finally come to personal conclusions
that we can gain the perspective of the others
and know and understand that illusion
is sometimes
just simple
reality

Go To Hell!

By: Author Renee' Drummond-Brown

Restore
that blind mans'
sight.
Give
that murderer
a second chance
at life.

Take away
those drugs.
Mature
that hooligan thug.
Feed
that crack baby.
Addiction
to bondage
minus
the subjugation
of slavery.

Black lives matter?
Yeah right!
If not here;
then where?
Definitely,
in the
hereafter.

Bang; bang
shoot 'em' dead
an' let
that piece of steel
be still;
and/or
"Go to Hell"
die 'tryin'
if
you will.

Dedicated to: *Dead is as dead does ('piece' be 'steel'.)*

A B.A.D. poem

Half Past 'y'OUR' Time

By: Author Renee' Drummond-Brown

I rehearsed
this line
'JUS'
one
more
time.
An'
until
we met Nino,
my sun
had a
restricted
shine.

Then,
you
'came'
along
an
farsighted
the shade
from
thine eyes.

Then,
my heart
sung songs
sang
out
of time.

Then,
I drank
Patti's
magnolia wine;
seasoned.
Yeah;
out of
'y'OUR'
rare
unfashionable
'vintage'd'
time.

Then,
I thirsted
no more.
Half past
'y'OUR' time.

Dedicated to: *C.N.B. Sr.*

A B.A.D. Poem

Happy "Dead-Beat" Dad's Day!

By: Author Renee' Drummond–Brown

You were
her
one night stand.
Ditched her;
as only
a sum bag
can!

9 months
later
a son
an'
daughter
came.
Your thoughts
"twins, they ain't mine!"
Her's
"what a low down dirty
shame."

'Lookin'
'jus'
like 'you' replenished
the earth.

Now
they're
all
grown
No child support
'EVER'
shown.
Spent most of your time
locked away.
An'
have
nerve
as they
graduate
to put
a smile
on your
fake, fake
face.
Here's to you
Farther
of the year
Happy "Dead-Beat" Dad's Day!

Dedicated to: *MAURY. HE IS THE FATHER!*

A B.A.D. Poem

HAPPY BIRTHDAY SUSAN JOYNER-STUMPF!

By: Author Renee' Drummond–Brown

Susan, Webster's describes you:
A
"native crystalline carbon that is the hardest known mineral that is usually nearly colorless, that when transparent and free from flaws is highly valued as a precious stone, and that is used industrially especially as an abrasive." (Webster's M., pg.345)
You come on the scene ma lady dropping sum hard prolific rhymes, an' sistah gal 'YOU KNOW' PRECISELY…JUST… what I mean! For no reason at all. I see the native crystalline in the origin your rhythm so eloquently speaks. NO carbon copy can duplicate the tunes your words so articulately speaks. A colorless rainbow is what you clarify in your penned words; while others talk the talk, you walk the walk AN' IT for sure shows within 'your' matchless gems an God's colorful rainbow.

Your heart is transparent FREE from flaws. A sophisticated lady! Highly valued, especially, from us all. Yeah, you answered Face Books' call an' never do you say no…No, not to one; one at all.
So IF…I've never told you before. I love you Susan Joyner-Stumpf, even if… there were sum minor flaws. But no not your precious stone…
Your Abrasiveness at times is to get us all through our bumps in the road an' some of these industrial poetic blues we so choose to think an' INK. I see you my sister. I DO SEE YOU and YOU are not alone. Someone once said "A diamond IZ a girlz best friend" and so, we thank you Susan for being OUR Semi precious stone!

All-in-all
SUSAN JOYNER-STUMPF
YOU
sister gal, have been my/our
DIAMOND IN THE ROUGH!

Dedicated to: My rock and POETIC sistah Susan Joyner-Stumpf.

A RocDeeRay Poem

Have It Your Way

By: Author Renee' Drummond–Brown

Two all-beef prose
Special words
Literature
Consonance
Poetry
Onomatopoeia
on a
Stanza seed bun.

Dedicated To: *You Deserve a Break Today*

A B.A.D. Poem

TRACEY ROBERSON

Aug. 20 2013

I am a Published Author of Poetry /Spoken Word Artist
I currently am working on a Spoken Word CD.
My Passion and gift is putting myself into situations and then writing about them,
I have been writing since 2000, after going thru some rough times, I was inspired by a good friend to
let my anger and pain out by writing.
I was born and raised in Ohio. I currently Reside in Pittsburgh Pa. with my 4 children which 3 are
now grown. I am an Army Veteran, and work For a School district.
My work is written with belief that I will touch someone and they will realize they are not alone.
Welcome to PoeticT World Lyfe remember Live Love Never Judge

Have You Seen Her

By: Author Tracey Roberson

I c u watchin me
Wondering y u r staring at me
Lookin deep with in my mind
Deep within my soul
Do u c what I c My heart reaps
of so much sorrow pain
With no self-control
Yet u wonder y I am so cold
Deep within I cry I scream
I shout I want to be free
from this agony and distress
If only u knew the hidden scars
u would no longer judge me
u wouldn't have tried to change me
if only u looked beyond the physical distraction
u might have seen the inner beauty
U might have chosen to love me
Y I cried out your name
I did my very best
U choose to abuse me every day of my life
Eyes black n blue u criticized me
Accused me that my love was not true

I thought she might hide
as you stole her confidence and pride
But then I remembered the words of Mya Angelou
playin thru my mind as I repeated time after time
I must rise with every breathe every piece of strength I ever had
she decided to live
prepared for the fight she looked to God
and fought for this thing called Lyfe
And today she stands to say I survived this thing called lyfe
A Solider of a War that not many Survive
The kujichagulia she has gained
knowing The Nia she must strive 4 the ultimate test
with Imani she pulled thru the ultimate test
with her Umoja and Kuumba she has been blessed
with that wonderful world of Success
She conquered that devastating Past
Enjoyin the love of Lyfe and the Blessing of Success
Again I ask have U seen her

ANNA FLETCHER

Based in Plymouth, UK, with a professional and academic background in Special Educational Needs, Anna is a single parent to her teenage son who has autism, ADHD and learning difficulties. Anna enjoys writing poems and plays with a point; designed to boost the wellbeing of others as well as to raise awareness of autism and other mental health conditions. Anna is delighted to be contributing to today's poetry, viewing poetry as a beautiful and unique form of communication, a gift from the heart to the heart of others, whatever the topic.

Haven

Scrimped and saved
on a single parents wage,
turned those tired working hours
into quality time for us
and I took us to the sea.
Oh, how proud that I did this for us!
But on arrival, that pride
turned with the tide
into loneliness and doubt
and 'how'd we end up here'?
Just the two of us
on a family holiday,
me, minus a husband,
you, without your daddy.
But we found our happiness
there on the shoreline
where the sea kissed our toes
and gave us a blank canvas.
You skipped stones
I searched the horizon
and willed the moon's magic
to bring us a catch.

His Race Is Given To The Strong

By: Author Renee' Drummond–Brown

Father,
often times
'You'
give 'one'
entirely
'TOO' 'TOO'
'TOO' 'MUCH'
to bear.
While, others
seem not
to have a care.

WHY?

My child,
My race
is given
to the
strong.
Just trust Me;
Be still.
And know,
I AM HERE.

Dedicated to: *My poetic sister Author Krista Vowell Clark*

A B.A.D. Poem

HOLD UP WAIT A MINUTE

By: Author Renee' Drummond-Brown

Hold up
wait
a minute
let me
put 'sum'
poetry
in it!

He;
fine
as can be.
Red bone,
an'
lean.
Standing,
'ALL' but
6ft. 3.
'Sportin''
'dat' brim.
Man,
it 'sho' 'nuff'
look good
on him!
Hmm,
not to mention
them ribs.

Yeah,
I know a 6 pack
when I see one.
And that one's
'Sho' 'nuff'
'NOT'
made in China
but 'RATHER'
earned
'AT'
an 'expensive'
'kindda'
gym!

His dress;
My Lord~~~
Wicked.
From the north, east, south
AND YES
THE
WILD WILD WEST!!!
Expensive alligator shoes;
'matchin' wallet
'wit'
'NO' food stamps
'HOLLA'!

Hold up
wait

a minute
let me
put 'sum'
TRIFLING
in it!

Yeah,
He fine
as can be.
NOT BAD
for a 'BUM'
she
collected off
them streets.
'Puttin' him
'ov'r'
her 'kidzs'.
AND WHOSE WATCHING HIM
AS THEM
'KIDDIES' SLEEP?

'Kidzs' ain't got
no shoes,
dirty draws,
crusty eyes
and
'matchin' feet
too.
But, he clean

as a tack.
'drivin' her ride;
while she an' her 'kidzs'
'WALKIN' round
bare back!

Hold up
wait
a minute
let me
put 'sum'
EDUCATION
in it!

Hefty
13 gallon
trash bags
are tough
as can be.
Lysol your house down gal;
better yet
use 'sum' Febreze
and Clorox
with
EXTRA, EXTRA, EXTRA
bleach.
'REMEMBER',
get your car keys,
credit cards too,
alarm' your house down.

You know what is 'IZ'!
You 'KNOW EXACTLY'
what you must do!
Give him them clothes
SO,
the spirit
moves on
an' goes
into the next game
cause that's all
he 'knowz'.
NOW
look at your kids
face;
with such laughter
in their
clean home.
as the garbage 'IZ' taken out
of you
and your 'kidzs'
throne!

Hold up
wait a minute;
when they say
"'lookie' 'lookie' here;
let me holla at you"
TELL THEM
"STEP ASIDE
I'M 'COMIN' THROUGH

NO!
AIN'T GOT NO
HOUSE
CAR
FOOD STAMPS
GYM
AND/OR
CLOTHES
FOR YOU!
And ladies
Til' they put a ring on it~~~
Don't you
'EVER'
forget it!

Hold up
wait
a minute
I JUS PUT
'sum'
'Renee's Poems with Wings are Words in Flight"
in it!
Didn't I do it?

Hold up
wait
a minute
I think
My God
'jus'
brought you through it!
Won't 'HE' do it?

Dedicated to: *'Lookie' 'lookie' here; let me 'holla' at you for a minute! WALK ON BY (Isaac Hayes).*

A B.A.D. Poem

Hopscotch

By: Author Renee' Drummond-Brown

One, two;
a 'girlz'
'gotta' do
what
a 'girlz'
'gotta'
do.

Three. Four;
'Word' says
"For a whore is a deep ditch;
and a
strange woman
is
a narrow pit"
(Proverbs 23:27 KJV.)
'Nevatheless'
a whore
is forever
a whore.
AND
'neva'
'eva'
forget!

Five, six;
she picked
up
a trick.

Seven, eight;
for her
an' Joe
the penalty's'
great.

Nine, ten;
in hindsight,
'they'd'
'do it'
again
and
again
and
again.

Eleven, twelve;
JUDGEMENT
sends them
straight
to hell!
Hopscotch anyone?
Nightwalkers
don't ask;
and
certainly
don't
tell…

Dedicated to: *Hey Joe(s); 'wanna' give it a go?*

A B.A.D. Poem

How Deep is 'Y'our' Love?

By: Author Renee' Drummond-Brown

My love
runs
'ev'r'
so deep.
When I
fall;
I fall
hard.
When I
love;
yeah,
'dat's' right,
I love
for keeps.

So,
you get
1
time
to do me
an' 'when'
you do;

REMEMBER THIS
I wipe
my feet.
Shake
the dust,
from
my heels.
An'
'NEVER'
look back at you.
So,
read this
and
weep.

Dedicated to: *Oceanic deep.*

A B.A.D. Poem

How Do You Plead? Guilty as Charged!

By: Author Renee' Drummond-Brown

'Lookin' back
on
Calvary…
I'm
guilty
of
treason.

I
disserted
THEE;
like
a two headed
snake,
rest
assure;
one end
bites
while
the other end
flees!

Dedicated to: *All rise!*

A B.A.D. Poem

HOW 'WE' GOT 'OV'R'?

By: Author Renee' Drummond-Brown

How did we go
from
'plantin''
a garden
an' 'makin'
'THE FIRST'
family;
not Obama's,
but,
'wit'
a dad,
and
a
mom
called
Eve?

How did we go
from
'crossin',
'wit' a man
named
Moses
an'
'da' help
of Aaron;

a
Red Sea?

How did we go
from
wondering
400+ years
in
an' out
of
desert lands
an' thINK
we'd 'ever'
be free?

How did we go
from
'AFRICA'
NOT 'EVEN' KNOWING
MOMMA
'LUCY';
into,
out of
and
'BACK'
into
slavery?

How did we go
From
The Civil Rights Movement
'wit'
a King
AND
'THE KING'
OF
'ALL' KINGS?

How did we go
from
racism,
discrimination,
segregation,
oppression,
retaliation
to
amnesia
to
obliviousness
to
'TOTAL'
'TOTAL'
loss
of
'ANY'
recollection
of
memory?

How did we go
from
rioting
in 'dem'
streets,
through genocide
to worrying
about
'SUM'
nails
and hair
on fleek?

How did we go
from
welfare
to
Doctorate
Degrees
back to
stupidity?

How did we go
from
a man
or
A 'MAN'

In 'OUR' house
to putting
him
or 'HIM'
in 'dem'
streets?

How did we go
From
raising
'OUR'
children's
children's
children
to
'DEM'
little kids
raising
'THEIR'
'VERY YOUNG'
Grammy's?

How did we go
from
our kids
being
'mannerable'
YES MAM-NO SIR.

to
selling dope,
shooting
one another,
LOSS OF HOPE,
robbing
'grandma's'
'WHO RAISED THEM',
In
BROAD DAYLIGHT,
WITH
WITNESSES,
On
'OUR'
VERY OWN
so called…
city streets!!!

BUT THEN AGAIN
'WE'
DID
'HANG'
AN INNOCENT
MAN
ON A TREE,
AND YELLED,
"CRICIFY THEE" (us.)
While He,
compassionately
prayed

Father
forgive
thee.

Cause 'dats'
how 'WE' roll.
Won't 'WE" do it?
Won't 'WE' do it?

Dedicated to: *That's how* **'WE' GOT OV'R'?**

A B.A.D. Poem

HOW YOU LIKE 'him' NOW?

By: Author Renee' Drummond-Brown

'YOU'
was
the other
woman.
Until
'YOU'
became
his 'LIE'.
I mean
wife.
Now
he's
'cheatin''
on
you.
An'
you
got
the nerve
to
cry,
rant
and ask
why?

His
'ORDAINED'
wife
wants to know:
HOW YOU LIKE 'him' NOW?

Dedicated to: *Cheaters 'NEVER' win an' winners never lose!!!*
A B.A.D. Poem

SARAH ITO

Sarah Ito is an actress who has appeared in several major motion pictures and music videos. She is a published novelist, essayist, poet and blogger. She lives in Brooklyn, New York.

I Am Fiction

By: Author Sarah Ito

I did not die
Nor pass away
I was deleted.
I never lived
Nor drew a breath
I was invented.
I did not love
Nor break a heart
I was imagined.
I did not speak
Nor hear your words
I was written.
I did not age
Nor ever will
I am fiction.

I Believe I Can Fly

By: Author Renee' Drummond–Brown

Finally got my wings;
long
looong
OVER-DUE.
No-one
gave me
'em'.
Somehow
they 'jus' grew.
In fact,
they came clipped;
with a
disability
attached.
'BLACK'
missing feathers
'N'
all
(that lack).

'Nevatheless'…
I believe
my writing prose
still
heeds
her call(s).
I believe I can fly
yall.
For the love of poetry
If 'nothin' else;
lest
I fall.

Dedicated: *Incapacitated wings; that be me.*

A B.A.D. Poem

MICHAEL LEE JOHNSON

Michael Lee Johnson lived ten years in Canada during the Vietnam era. Today he is a poet, freelance writer, amateur photographer, and small business owner in Itasca, Illinois. Mr. Johnson published in more than 930 publications, his poems have appeared in 33 countries, he edits, publishes 10 different poetry sites. *He has been nominated **2 Pushcart Prize awards for poetry 2015 & Best of the Net 2016.** 134 poetry videos on YouTube: <u>https://www.youtube.com/user/poetrymanusa/videos</u>. He is the Editor-in-chief of anthology, Moonlight Dreamers of Yellow Haze: <u>http://www.amazon.com/dp/1530456762</u> A second poetry anthology, Dandelion in a Vase of Roses, Editor-in-chief, Michael Lee Johnson, is now available here: <u>http://www.amazon.com/dp/1545352089</u>.*

I Edit my Life

By: Author Michael Lee Johnson

I edit my life
clothesline pins & clips
hang to dry,
dirty laundry,
I turn poetic hedonistic
in my early 70's
reviewing the joys
and the sorrows
of my journey.
I find myself wanting
a new review, a new product,
a new time machine,
a new internet space,
a new planet where
we small, wee creative
creatures can grow.

I Wuz Born Not to Know?

By Author: Renee' B. Drummond-Brown

Who
I wuz?
What
prolific gift I have?
Where
I am going?
When
will I die?
Why
I'm made in His image?
And..
How
I got ov'r
in such hard-troublesome times?

And...
I wuz born not to ask, Him
who, what, where, when, how and/or ev'n why?

But I know that I know
Whose
I am.
What
I'll write.
Where

I'm going.
When
I'll die.
Why
I'm black.
And/or…
How
He got me ov'r.

I wuz born not to know?
But…
searched out
5 w's
along this HARD journey-way
THIS
FOR CERTAIN I DO KNOW.

Dedicated to: You can't touch this.

A RocDeeRay Poem

I'M MAD AS HELL!

By: Author Renee' Drummond-Brown

I'm mad as hell!

Oh!
You're shocked,
I said that!
Well,
I didn't 'utter'
'IT'
nor,
did I stutter
'IT'.
So,
I'll repeat 'IT'
again:
I'M MAD AS HELL,
for the dope
'WE ALLOW'
Our 'ADULT' kids to sell;
right
out of 'OUR' communities
and home.
Let's not get stupid,
an' act
as though

'WE'
'DON'T'
'KNOW'!

When in fact,
you got,
an 'ADULT' child
'livin' at home,
no school, nadda job,
sleeping-beauty
all day,
'WITH "EXTRA" NICKLES TO LOAN',
'IN "YOUR" HOUSE'
til dark.
Waiting,
lurking
to go out,
in the middle
of the
night;
selling,
shooting
and
free basting it up.
Then,
'WHEN'
they get shot.
"Oh my God"
the world must stop!

You're caught
off guard,
and have nerve
to be
ever so, distraught!!!
Until,
the T.V cameras come your way
offering you
15 minutes
of fame,
to explain,
how he/she
did
absolutely 'NOTHING'
to anyone,
and you simply can't understand,
who, what, where when and why they're shot!
Afterall,
it blows your mind,
cause they're
just
a victim
of circumstance;
caught,
at the wrong place,
at the wrong time???

First, comes the vigils.
Lest we forget
the shooters usually

standing
right there;
with 'sum' nerve,
and
it is
of course,
his or her best friend;
offering, mom
and family
their condolences,
and even
willing
to pay for the funeral expense.

10 people or more witness
the shooting
but 'NO-ONE'
see's
a 'thang'!
The difference
bout 'our' 'whineos', dope fiends
an' dealers;
back in the day,
they snatched 'ya' up
an' told us
"Baby,
don't be like me.

'YOU'
'gotta' stay away
from this junk!"

Naw,
not you;
new and improved parents.
You say,
"gotta get 'dat'
paper, paper, paper
come what may!"
Only then,
it becomes a generational curse
to the rest
of the
siblings
still living
at home.

Party City stores
'loves'
to see you come
To get your balloons and T-shirts made
for the quote-un-quote
victims mom.
Only she don't profit a dime.
All mom knows
is
teddy bears an' cards were sent,

candles were burnt,
and several people had their
T-shirts on
to be uniformed
as one
for the pain, injustices
and hurt done.

But,
what they 'gotta' understand,
Satan offers free flames
and as far as the helium
balloons
on the rise;
The Cannon of Scripture
doesn't except that
'kindda' sacrifice.
So they pop mid air
and never reach the firmaments.
I'M STILL MAD AS HELL!
I swear
I am.

I love you parents
and
I love your 'ADULT' kids.
But we
as a people
'gotta' do

much better than this
an'
'STOP'
turning a blind eye
and
bowing 'OUR' heads,
to what 'We 'KNOW'
is wrong;
let's get real here
and call true violence
'EXACTLY'
what it is.

First, we took God out of our homes.
Next, we removed
the Scriptures from schools.
Then,
the natural fathers had to be-gone, too.
That left the 'ADULT' kids
'FREE REIGN'
OF THE HOUSE
and ultimately
RAISING
THEIR MOMS;
who sees
absolutely no wrong

in their 'grown' daughters
and/or sons!!!

If this poem describes your 'ADULT' kids.
PUT 'EM' OUT
'LIKE YESTERDAY',
YEAH,
I DID NOT STUTTER;
THAT IS
WHAT I SAID.
PUT 'EM' OUT
AN' SAVE
THE REST OF THE UNDERAGE SIBBLINGS
WHO STILL RESIDE THERE.
AND IF,
THEY WON'T GO
YOU MOVE
ON TOMORROW!

Remember,
one bad apple
spoils the whole bunch
and we need
to make them flee.
Cause I don't know
bout you
but
"I'M MAD AS HELL"

at this infectious disease
infecting
our innocent children
and
'OUR' communities!

Note* This poem is in no way to say to give up on your 'child' in need of, and/or seeking help for a drug problem. This poem is rather an expression of the love of a mother and/ or father that 'MUST' take a stand when an 'adult' child has taken over their home and has no desire to get help. 'WE ALL' HAVE TO GET "MAD AS HELL" and stop this nonsense that we know to be true. I don't know about you, but I'm sick and tired, especially for the innocent children who have to live with this drama within their community!

Dedicated to: *The 'NOT' so innocent parents.*

A B.A.D. Poem

In The Back of My Mind

By: Author Renee' Drummond-Brown

I went to
The New
Jerusalem;
in the back
of my mind
and saw
Momma,
and
my brother's
sweetest
gentle smile.

On bended knees,
holding
onto
His hem,
she said,
like her Father,
touch me not.
Now go back.

Don't fret.
Your times
not up yet.
Care
for 'your' family
an' wait
till God calls you home;
taking from you,
'HIS'
last breath.

Dedicated to: *B.A.D. and S.C. D.*

A B.A.D. Poem

JEAN MORSE

Infinity

By: Author Jean Morse

Can I
comprehend it?
Wrap my head
around it.
Never ending.
Looking up,
at the heavens;
really?

INK Vows

By: Author Renee' Drummond-Brown

I, Author Renee' Drummond-Brown
pen you,
to be
my lawfully wedded poem,
to have and to hold,
from this day forward,
for blues,
for rhythm & rhyme,
for literature,
for narrative,
in writers block and in personification,
until
INK
do us part.

Dedicated to: *I do!!!*

A B.A.D. Poem

'IZ'

By: Author Renee' Drummond-Brown

Hurt
'IZ' all she knew.
Dirt
'IZ' is all He gained.
Pain
'IZ' all she grew.
Reign
'IZ' His domain.

Dedicated: Love 'IZ' not there.
A B.A.D. Poem

KEN ALLAN DRONSFIELD

Ken Allan Dronsfield is a published poet from New Hampshire, now residing in Oklahoma. He loves thunderstorms! His published work can be found in reviews, journals, magazines, and anthologies throughout the web and in print venues. His poetry has been nominated for two Pushcart Prize Awards and the Best of the Net for 2016.

Jacob Swam the River

By: Author Ken Allan Dronsfield

Motley dressed
with holy socks
matching shoes
gray thinning hair
lives by the bridge
last ate on Sunday
fought in Vietnam
hides in plain sight
raucous lost dreams
fire and icy breath
in spite, death calls
peace finally found
a cold November day
socks, shoes unlaced
placed upon the bank
his war finally ends,
Jacob swam the river.

JAZZ Don't Mean A 'Thang' if Rhythm and Blues Ain't Got that 'Swang'

By: Author Renee' Drummond-Brown

Saturday
the dusk
of dew;
63.

~~~

Naw cuz,
'twaz'
1961

~~~

or
'wuzn't' it
62?
˜ ˜ ˜

'Anywho'
>>>
skipped us
'sum'
SERIOUS
school.
<<<
Mabey
it twas'
afternoon?

In the
black
Southern
comfort sun.
Or
'wuzn't' it
Southern comfort
us 'wuz'
'drankin' on?
???

WHO KNEW?
we'd
beg
borrow

an'
stole
us
some fun?

Down
at the
Juke joint;
'smokin''
on
tobacco,
'eaten''
'dem''
pork 'rhymes'.
Naaa!
'Dats''
a lie!
We 'wuz''
'chewin''
on
'sum''
fried CAT.
Fish
'dat''
'IZ'???

Chitterlings
an' OH' kale,
mustard greens
naw
dayze' steamed,

ham hock
neck-bones
'wit' them
negro beans
an'
simply red
rice.
Spinach AIN't there!
Now
'dats'
mighty fine of you
and
'sum'
cornbread
sounds
'kinda' nice.
~~~
Might add…
~~~
Christianly
too.

Grease 'poppin'
foot 'stompin'
shaking off
calories
and
them there blues.

'Groovin'
to sounds of

herbie hancock
muddy waters
little walter
miles davis
louis armstrong
dizz gillespie
duke ellington
john coltrane
an
lest we forget
charlie parker
too.
ROLL CALL:
They don't get A capitol?
'Naw'
daze ain't
hardly
'IMPO'TANT'
just 'acktin'
'sum'
black fools!!!

But
'dayz' 'due'
⁓⁓⁓
THIS TIME
⁓⁓⁓
get a pass;
⁓⁓⁓
unlike,
⁓⁓⁓

Me
an' You!!!

Aw,
now 'dat' there's
'sum'
Cannon
'kinda'
"Good News"
"be for real"
JAZZ, Rhythm, and Blues!
Oh my!!!
Naw,
dorothy and toto
'wuzan't'
hardly
there too.
There's no place like home though
or
'skippin' us
'sum' school;
cross
the railroad tracks,
back
in
the neck of the woods
AKA
OZ
and/or
DA'

Juke Joint.
UNDERSTOOD?

harold melvin,
&
the blue notes
'WUZ' THEY THERE TOO?
Alright; alright
If you don't know me
by now
You 'betta' ask 'sumbody'
bout my poetry~~~
RENEE'S POEMS WITH WINGS ARE 'FOREVA'
WORDS IN FLIGHT!!!

SHE'S ONE
JAZZY BABE,
and yezzz'
JAZZ
don't mean A 'thang'
if
Rhythm and Blues
ain't got
that 'swang'!!!

Dedicated to: *You 'betta' ask 'sumbody' 'bout' my poetry~~~*
RENEE'S POEMS WITH WINGS ARE WORDS IN FLIGHT!!!

A B.A.D. Poem

Lady Sang the Blues

By: Author Renee' Drummond-Brown

Now
'dat' dears'
'sum'
real good
news!
Ain't no way
'dat'
sanctified lady
can have
anybody's blues!!!
Say it ain't so?

Oh' no!!!
Sustah sang!

No it ain't.
Trouble in her way
she's got the blues
real BAD
to sang.
Billie Holiday's
no
ole' school fool.
Yeah,
She knew
just
what to do.
'Dem' dear haves
an'
'dem' dear don'ts'
Some say
you can
Billie Holiday
sang
you won't.
True 'dat'.

Who orchestrated
this mess?
God bless the child
who got his own?
Billie's
trumpet man

played on
an'
the Saxophone,
well
joined in
"Lets get it on."
No it didn't
'dats'
Marvin Gaye's
ol' song
and/or
Rev. Al Green
on 'da'
organ
naw,
I think it 'twuz'
the guitar
'whicheva'
'makin' his scene.
You know
what I mean.
Stevie
wonders bout
the harmonica and bongos'
'dat'
string along;
an'
that piano
that stretches
Alicia's key of C
to her tune

of
a different sound.
Oh' no
this is so
very wrong!
Why can't
the pianist
like
rodney king
just
get along
and beat
to the drum(mond)
of ev'rybody else's
song?

She's of
a different world
'wit'
no class,
absolutely
no taste
a faceless woman
without
a face,
what
an embarrassment;
sheer elegance
of poetry
at its best
disgrace.

Broken
lil' rich girl;
who knew?
Jazz, Rhythm and Blues;
oh my.
Truth be told,
Iz'
be the lady,
Billies'
'sangin' bout
'wit'
dem' dear blues.
Who knew?
Billie knew
way before
my time
'dats' who.
Yeah,
I got the blues
I got 'em'
BAD…
True 'dat'
and so
do you.

Dedicated to: *Jazz, Rhythm and Blues; who knew? Billie 'dats who.*

A B.A.D. poem

KWELI

Kweli is a spoken word artiste and writer from Accra Ghana, West Africa who tries to write from the heart. Kweli started writing as a form of therapy to deal with depression, anger and pain but now try to use his writing to inspire others. Kweli has three singles out on SoundCloud.com. It is his dream to one day perform the perfect spoken word piece that will elicit smiles, laughter, tears and hope.

*Twitter: @Kweli_*

*Instagram: @Kwlie_*

FaceBook: Efo Kweli

Lay Me To Rest

By: Author Kweli

Lay my emotions to rest. On this alter I built with my heart breaks
Do not weep for the death of my emotions, rejoice and remember
The fond memories we shared.

Lay my emotions to rest, on this holy ground which have been watered
By the storms of my life. Do not pity my lose. Do not rail against the injustice,
Smile and remember the good times.

My heart is laid bare, my heart beat is still, and my breath is no more
Love has deserted me. Who do I turn to? In my moment of
Hopelessness, who will define hope for me?

The chapter is closed, the rest of the story is left untold, I will
Never again know what happy is. Lay my emotions to rest,
On this flaming pyre I built from the hurt and disappointments
I have endured.
Lay me to rest and sing a somber hymn for love lost

Letter To Mandela

By: Author – Ngozi Olivia Osuoha

Things are falling apart
Homes they vow to thwart,
We are no longer at ease
Lives they always erase,
It is not the arrow of God
But the wickedness of a god,
They have killed UBUNTU

You fiercely fought apartheid
And your destiny untied,
Your long walk to freedom
Was an act of wisdom,
The audacity of hope
Inspired in order to cope,
They just killed UBUNTU.

Frying people like potato
May cause nightfall in Soweto,
The message of Mandela
Preaches no violence for Madiba,
The dream of your fathers
Contributed to your prison diary,
Where then is UBUNTU?

There was a country
With half of a yellow sun
Almost wiped by gun
By an adverse enfrontery,
A victim of circumstance
Searching for greener pasture,
UBUNTU is murdered.

Papa Africa, call them to order
Enough is enough.

#KILLING OF STRANGERS IS UNAFRICAN

LETTER TO MY TEACHER

By: Author – Ngozi Olivia Osuoha

Haggard; you were a digger
Mustard; your faith was bigger,
You can never be forgotten
My teacher, never to rotten
Dead; you are a legend
Alive; you are a friend,
Thank you, thank you.

Disrespect walked out of class
Ignorance walked into glass,
Indiscipline expected you to cry
Inexperience left himself dry,
Hatred did you waylay
Stubbornness forgot payday,
On their behalf; forgive.

Your old school hair, they pocked
Your torn trousers, they mocked,
Childishness laughed at your shoes
Brutality stepped on your toes,
Foolishness played you games
Stupidity called you names,
Never mind, forgive.

Disobedience always did wrong
Outlaw bullied the young,
Freedom misused his fees
Abject poverty stung by bees,
Mischief came for a fight
Weapons consumed your night,
Yet committed; thank you.

They knew you were hungry
Knew not you were a laundry,
They knew you were thirsty
So they became very nasty,
For all they did dramatize
On their behalf, I apologize
Forgive, thank you.

Now I fully understand
All you wanted to withstand,
I thought it was wickedness
But you built me for wilderness,
I appreciate the punishment
It was for a sound development,
Thank you, thank you.

Thank you for the manual labour
It added my strength; flavour
For answered questions, thank you
For unanswered ones, thank you
For each assignment, thank you
For each flogging, thank you
For everything, thank you.

I can now comprehend
Why you could not pretend,
You were a role model
Wanted me, a supermodel,
It was a royal target
You vowed; no regret
Thank you, thank you.

If I never held the chalk
If I never did the long walk,
If you were not my teacher
If you never turned a preacher,
If you never saw me green
Wonder, I would have been,
Perhaps, a terrible NUISANCE

DEDICATED TO TEACHERS WORLDWIDE ESPECIALLY TO MY PARENTS YOU ARE INCREDIBLE

Liar, Liar; Your Pants Are on Fire!

By: Author Renee' Drummond-Brown

My eyes
see(N)
you cheat.
You say
it 'wazant' me!

OK SHAGGY,
an'
RIK-ROK,
you take me
for a fool.
I say
it was;
you say,
it 'wazant' you!
Do I look like
Scooby Doo
to you?

I see(N)
you 'wit' her
'walkin'
down the street.
On
your 'lyin' lips,

you (both) say
the pavements
concrete.

I see(N) her
child
HUN.
'Lookin' 'JUS'
like you.
But...
you an' Billie-Jean say
the 'kidzs' not your son!

An' that's quite OK,
'FOR SURE';
cause
neither 'IZ'
the 'children'
you pay me
child support
for.

Dedicated to: *Liar, Liar; Both 'OUR' Pants Are on Fire!*

A B.A.D. Poem

Metamorphosis

By: Author Renee' Drummond-Brown

Milkweed leaf, began her egg stage.
'Creepin' caterpillars came to her aide.
Pupa 'sang' her puberty in vain.
Black butterfly's cycle's her metamorphosis reign.

Dedicated to: (Terri, Kia, Dee-Dee, Raven and Anaija) Fly dark girls fly.

A B.A.D. Poem

Mirrors

By: Author Renee' Drummond-Brown

Smoking glass
Cracks
The fairest of all

Author Renee' B. Drummond-Brown

Dedicated to: *Imagery*

A B.A. D. Poem

Money, Money, Money, Money…Money!

By: Author Renee' Drummond-Brown

$itting here
Gra$ping
time;
$he got
her mind
on
her money
and
her money

on
her rhyme$.

Light$,
water,
and
ga$ off;
$econd hand
$moke too.
'HOLEY, HOLEY, HOLEY'
jean$ on;
'waaay'
too $mall.
What
a $ick
broke
'kinda' joke?
And
what'$
a gal
to do?

'$portin'
you gue$$ed
right
a ra$pberry
beret; I $wear.
'Lookin' fre$h
'talkin' bout

Fre$h prince
of Belair
'kinda' fre$h.
Mighty fine
of her
'dreamin''
'$um'
big 'thang$'.
'Livin' off
a dime.

$hhhh;
only
don't $ay
welfare;
cau$e $he
don't
like
the like$
of 'THAT'
kind!

On
one accord
with
her Lord.
But..
that'$ all,
in the ghetto,

$he
can afford!
'Kinda' dope.
Fal$etto dreams.
No hope.

he' forever
u$e
to the word$
NO.
NO WAY.
And
NOPE!

Project$
can't hold
a good woman down!
Naw,
not 'wit'
her
'$aditty' $uburban, $tubborn
'kinda' rich
'kinda' uppity mind;
laced
with
fine chee$e,
Caviar,
Champagne ta$te
and 'thee'

rare$t
of
fine$t,
bottled wine.
All for
you gue$$ed right;
what $he
can afford.
$1.99.

Yep,
the dollar tree $tore.
Wig $tore.
And
nail $hops too;
got all
her
need$ met
at one
$TOP
$hop
till $he
drop!!!

$he's broke baby'.
But baby
got game.
Downtown
5th Avenue

'EVEN'
know$ her
by name.
$he dream$
big thang$.
1787
Chateau Margaux
or
Margo.
Whichever
is eaiet
for you
to pronounce
and/or
$ay.
$500,000....
a pop
for
Gou^t de Diamant$
$2.07 mill
ion;
'dat' i$......
them$'
$ho' 'nuff'
'$um' diamond$$$
calculated
in her head.
Yeah,
a gal$
best friend.
But

for now,
$he Rock$!
cubic zirconia$'
in$tead.
Who knew?
Certainly
not you.
Only
'THE WELL TO DO';
DO.

$o, let me gue$$?
$he 'gotta'
knock off Gucci
too???
True 'dat'
True 'dat'.
But
$he $erves
THE ORIGINAL GOD
$o he'
ble$$ed
after-all; the fake diamond$, jewelry, wine an'
'dem' hoopty
Le' car$.

BUT
FOR GRACE,
HER
ORIGINAL GOD
IS NO
KNOCK OFF
by far!

Dedicated to: *You can't keep a good woman down!*

A B.A.D. Poem

Mother Knows Best

By: Author Renee' Drummond-Brown

Do
what you want.
Say
what you will.
The Father
knows
3 sides to every story.
HIS,
yours,
mine;
an' Lord knows
I've 'HAD'
my fill!

This is the part
I exit
stage right;
leaving you all
in the dust
like
a thief
in the night.
Following
the words
of
Angelou

"STILL
I RISE!"

Instead of sugar coating
all ones
white lies.
In the end;
It's best
to relinquish
'ALL' ties.

I've been hated by
the best
and loved
by few.
Mother knew best
and taught me
TO THINE "OWN" SELF
BE TRUE!
Truth be told,
I did a lot for you
and yours too…
but,
what have you done for me
lately?
And mines' too?

Dedicated to: *TO THINE SELF BE TRUE!*

A B.A.D. Poem

My INKfriends

By: Author Renee' Drummond-Brown

THIS
'ain't
my 'FIRST'
ring around
the rosy.
My pen

'COMES OUT'
the pocket
full
of
'POESY'.

I
INK
HARD!!!
Coming out
'THE GATE'
GANG 'BAGIN'
HOLLYWOOD
'SWANGIN'
'WIT'
'THE BIG DAWGZS'
or
like
Nicki Minaj;
I
DON'T
COME OUT
AT
ALL!

I ain't afraid
of
no ghost
(CEPT THE HOLY ONE).

Come against me
and my
pen
yes sir; yes sir,
'WILL'
'TAKE YOU'
STRAIGHT
'TO CHRUCH'.
Yeah,
I'll take you
there.
CAN I GET A WITNESS?
WON'T SHE DO IT?
WON'T SHE DO IT?
And the Staple Sangers sang
Amen.
Amen.

I've lived
'sum'
years.
Experience
has dealt me
'sum'
tears,
fear
and 'YES'
'ev'n'
judgmental
stares,

which taught me
a 'thang'
or 2
bout where
to cast
'ALL'
my cares.

I PUT MY MONEY
where my
'GRILLZ'
'iz'.
And
got my mind
on my
poems
and my
poems
on my
rhymes.
Dat's
'SO'
'fo' real
'FOR REAL'.
Alright.
Alright.

I'm
UNIQUELY

genuine.
ASK
MY PEN
or
INKfriends
and
you'll find
there's
Ecclesiastical
seasons
to
'ALL'
my
madness
and
scripted
BRAND of RHYMES!

Dedicated to:
Ask 'NOT' what your poetry can do for you; but, what your poetry can do for humanity.

A B.A.D. Poem

'Neva' Let 'Em' See 'YOU' Sweat

By: Author Renee' Drummond-Brown

I 'neva' slept
all
night long.
Went
to bed
at
the break of dawn.
Hives drew
all 'ov'r'
my face,
legs
an' arms.
But…
I 'neva'
'EVA'
let 'em'
see me
sweat
before
nights long.

No!
'Nadda' one!!
No!
Not at all!!!
I walk 'dem' floors;

for you my 'chile',
I prayed
'ALL'
night long.
Went to the Father
to
cast 'OUR' cares.
'Neva' let 'em' see you sweat
my dear.
No
'Nadda' tear.

Although,
I shed me
'sum'
healthy fears
before
morn.
I'll never forget
5/31/17,
as long
as I live hun!
WVU,
1:30 pm.
You came out
the gate 'swangin'
strong.
An' 'sustah' gal,
you--we,
earned 'THAT' crown.

Hail to the Queen(s)
or
Hell to the Queen(s)
which 'eva' mood I'm in
(LOL)!
CONGRATULATIONS
Dr.
Renee' Barbara-Ann Brown.
An 'wit' momma
by your side~~~
YOU BET.
Us 'sustah' gals
'gone'
turn this world
upside down.
An'
'neva' 'EVA' let 'em'
see us sweat!
Signed,
both Renee' Brown's.

Dedicated to: CONGRATULATIONS 'EARNING' Y'OUR' DOCTORATE DEGREE-I love you, mommy.

A B.A.D. Poem

No, Not One

By: Author Renee' Drummond–Brown

Don't need god(s).
Don't need a friend.
Just
in need of
a God
who'll
carry me
to
the end.

Dedicated to: *No, not one; but, I tell Him 'bout' my troubles.*

A B.A.D. Poem

'Nothin' But The 'Dawg' In Me!

By: Author Renee' Drummond-Brown

'WATCH'
them 'dawgz'
that 'brang'
a bone.
They usually
roam
home to home.
Always out
for trouble;
refusing
to let
one be
an'
leave you/well enough alone
bothering
'NO-ONE'!
They refuse
to
sit still;
carrying gossip
house
to house
at
'FREE'will.

Every-time
they appear;
they tell
you
what others
feel.
When
in fact,
they're too
illiterate
to know
that
'YOU'
know.
It's them
'branging'
and
carrying
their
'VERY OWN'
troublesome
bones!!!

Let 'em' lone,
ignore 'em'
immediately.
An'
I guarantee,
they'll go
roaming
an'
'barkin'
up
someone else's
tree
and believe
you me;
one day
it'll soon be
the 'WRONG'
'TREE'!

POEM NOTE* DON'T FORGET 'THE FATHER' IS THE 'TREE' OF LIFE!

Dedicated to: *Here doggy; doggie. 'Snoop', there it 'iz'!*

A B.A.D. Poem

242

One Monkey Don't 'STOP' No Show

By: Author Renee' Drummond-Brown

*You know
he laughed
when you left.
But then,
cried
to himself.*

*In front of
'his' 'boyz'
he
had to
play it
cool,
but alone
'KNEW'
he 'wuz'
THE BIGGEST FOOL;
to lose
a jewel
like you.*

Now,
you 'lookin'
all good;
'wit'
your new man.
An, he
'standin'
'wit'
his 'boyz';
'PROUD'
acting glad,
inside
feeling
mad, miserable and sad.
Knowing;
he lost
the best thing,
He'd
ever had.

Dedicated to: *Baby 'PLEASE' come back!!!*

A B.A.D. Poem

One Night Stand

By: *Author Renee' Drummond-Brown*

While
we're rolling
on
a river
Tina once
'sang'
"What's 'luv'
got to do
'wit' it?
'Jus'
'A'
second hand
emotion."
Not us…
You remember,
you
told me
you
loved me?
Or
wasn't it
my
poetic thoughts
of imaginings'
in
motion?

You moved
a million
hearts
of
unknown;
crossed
vast oceans
oh'
'dem'
Red Seas
within
this
great
so called
American Dream;
'wit'
grains
an'
'waves'
of 'luv'
as though
it may seem.

Your hello's
meant
bye.
If only
like Patti,
'I KNEW'

the first kiss said
goodbye;
I would've
kiss 'N' told
long ago
~ ~ ~
anyhow!

As you
exited
stage right;
'Encore'
'Encore'
I'll give you
a hand.
Clap, Clap.
'Cuz'
in my mind
you 'wuz'
THE ONE
In fruition,
I 'wuz'
'da'
one-night
stand.

Dedicated to: *Frankie, why do fools fall in 'luv'?*

A B.A.D. Poem

Paper Doll

By: Author Renee' Drummond-Brown

So very fragile,
flimsy,
delicate
an'
paper thin.

Easy to cut
an'
take advantage of
within.

Scissors
are definitely
no
fan, foe or friend.
Cause
She easily breaks,
tears
and/or
bends.

The clothes
dress her up;
but can't
stop the tears.
The stand
stands her up

But…
In scotch tape
she must
cast
her cares.

Brittle
on the inside
friable
to the touch.
Newspapers
talk
round
bout her
daily;
Tabloids
report
their hunch.

I got a premonition
paper dolls
aren't meant
to be cut.

Dedicated to:
All the Kings horses and all the Kings men; can't put a paper doll back together again.

A B.A.D. Poem

Patience

By: Author Renee' Drummond-Brown

I love you my children.
But,
my heart
belongs
to God.
I have even forsaken the Scriptures
in
an attempt
to give
to you
my all.

And even,
in giving my all,
I can't seem
to please.
So,
now
all that's left is tears,
fears,
and patience;
while dropping
to my knees!

Patience is endurance
under difficult
circumstance.

Which is
plain to see.
What was more difficult
than God,
allowing Jesus,
to have patience
with me
on Calvary?

I now
have to release you
to your rightful owner,
because you
were never mine.
And He alone,
will shape
and mold you
like He did
when turning waters
into wine.
(John 2)

My children,
your rightful owner
is none other
than God.
He'll take
something
out of nothing
and create
like he did

for Moses,
while using
only
a rod.

I realize
that it was God's precious time
that I gave you
from day
to day.
But,
I should have used the time more wisely
on patience,
and
allowing more time
to pray.

Because of this,
I now have to pray harder
in season and out when things look grim.
And even
pray some more
when times
are at their worst
and chances
look
very slim.

My children,
I can't operate
off of chance,

but rather
pure faith.
I'm begging you
Father,
please remove these tears,
fears,
pains
and
heartaches!

Like you asked your Father Jesus;
I now ask
Father, can you let this cup pass from me?

Be patient My child
with 'MY' children
in care of you,
as 'I' have
directed thee.

Did you forget the patience
that I had
with you
way back when?
Your forefathers crucified
My Only
Begotten Son
who died
for your
sins!

Yet,
in all
that has been done to Me;
I still have
patience
with you.
So,
when your children
get
at their ugliest,
do
as I do;
be patient,
and
wait on Me
to move!

Father you said
in
Ecclesiastes 3
You'll make everything beautiful
in time.
If my kids only knew;
for them,
I too,
would lay down
my life
with no
reason or rhyme.

Patience;

don't tempt me My child
to move
on your behalf,
because
I created thy word,
without
a blemish or blur.
"Her children arise up, and call her blessed; her husband also, and he praiseth her."
(Proverbs 31:28 KJV)

Satan you can't trick me
in giving up
on mine.
I'm gonna hold on
with patience
a little tighter,
until
God delivers
His children
in
His time!

Dedicated to: *For all who struggle with patience like me.*

A B.A.D. Poem

Pay The Piper

By: *Author Renee' Drummond-Brown*

Oh'
them lips;
start
a flame
in her
heart
with every
good-bye
kiss.

His heart,
plays
musical chairs
with
a burning desire;
like authentic
poetic
arts
contagious flames
lit
on fire.

His mind,
so
analytical,
an'
methodical.
No,
better yet
plain.
An' yet,
so unembellished
pulsates
her mind
like thunder
is
to rain
!!!!!!!!!!!!!!

His body;
'sho' 'nuff'
a brick;
6-pack
if you will.
So very built.
And yet,
just like
a glove
to mind;
it fits
yeah,
it fits
her kind.

His hands
so,
demonically
possessed
tore her away
from
existence;

the very
day,
they pronounced
her dead.
His
domestic
plight
strategically
crafted
misery
an' doomed her
the gates of Hell's;
eternity
strife.

Dedicated to: *She'll see you in Hell; you 'must' pay the piper.*
(DOMESTIC ABUSE AWARENESS)

A B.A.D. Poem

Playground(s) In My Mind

By: Author Renee' Drummond-Brown

When
I was a child,
I thought
as a child.
I spoke
like a child.
I acted
like a child;
just the same.
When
I became a
woman;
I put away fools
and them
childish games.

Dedicated to: *The Garden of Eden.*

A B.A.D. Poem

POETRY

By: *Author Renee' Drummond-Brown*

Poetic thoughts
Outweigh
Eternity
Time
Re-writes
Yesterday

Dedicated to: *Poetic thoughts*

A B.A.D. Poem

Promise You Won't Tell?

By: Author Renee' Drummond-Brown

I'm 'lettin'
you know;
my poetic
flow
'IZ'
so
'fo' real.
Cause
we
got
us
'sum'
secrets;
no-one
else
can hear.
$hhhhh.

Dedicated to: *C.N.B.*

A B.A.D. Poem

Say It Ain't So!

By: Author Renee' Drummond-Brown

Say It Ain't So!
'Sayin' he 'wanna'
study
to show himself approved
at
4:00
IN THE MORN!

Say It Ain't So!
He 'wanna' hide
you,
like a thief
in the night.
'SUMthin'
JUST
ain't
quite right!

Say It Ain't So!
He 'gotta'
wife an'kidzs'
who love him
' fo' 'sho'!

Say It Ain't So!
He 'gotta'
huge
following;
'turnin' their head(s);
acting
as though
they don't get it
'NOR'
do they really 'WANNA' know!

Say It Ain't So!
MR. PREACHER-MAN;
when exposed
'runnin' fast as you can
like
the gingerbread man.
'Cept'
you run your game
lil' faster
than Satan can.
(Catch that if you can, an' while you at it, put it in your pipe an' smoke it).

Say It Ain't So!
Heard
you moved on
to someone else;
to study
the word
at
4:00
in the morn!
We already know:
say It Ain't So!

Dedicated to: *Time don't heal all wounds (say It Ain't So)!*

A B.A.D. Poem

Send In The Clowns!

By: Author Renee' Drummond-Brown

Send in the clowns.
Makeup
so thick
MAC
don't
'ev'n'
want you
round.

Send in the clowns.
When you

dare
wear
short; shorts,
baby gal.
Introduce
those legs
an'
hair
to
'sum' Nair.

Send in the clowns.
Waving weave
high
in the air.
'Shakin''
'round';
like
its
natural hair.

Send in the clowns.
Baby 'needin''
pampers;
you need
'sum' nails.
While you
all
gelled up;

guess
who smells?

Send in the clowns,
the wannabee's.
'lookin' like
Christmas
in July;
artificial
trees'.
BLING; BLING.
Naw,
Baby Girl.
AIN'T 'NOTHIN' LIKE
THE REAL
'THANG'.
'Dems' 'sum'
cubic
zirconia's
AKA
diamond rings!

Send in the clowns.
Priorities
out of order;
life
one big
mess.
Selfies'

texting,
Face Book,
clothes;
'THE BEST DRESS'.
Lest
we forget
THE
cell phones
all come
before
life insurance.
And
one's own
death.

Send in the clowns.
I ain't
forgot
bout
Him.
He
'walkin'
round;
rotten teeth.
'Robbin'
jewelry stores,
'witta'
AKA
NELLY
smile.

NELLY
GOT
MONEY
for his
'GRILLZ'.
Your mouth
all day
longs'
'spinnin'.
You in the game
Playa; Playa.
'Lookin' like
you
' fo sho's'
'winnin'.

Send in the clowns.
Pants
'hangin' low.
'Bustin'
a sag.
Babies
ain't got
no shoes,
clothes
nor
food.
Playa; Playa
got
5 PAIR,

$400 dolla'
tennis-shoes.

Send in the clowns.
In 'dem' clubs;
you
'droppin'
'dollas'
like they
hot.
Let me guess;
credit scores
down?
Playa, Playa
real men
carry
Discover cards
round
town.

Send in the clowns.
I call 'em'
like
I 'SEE'
'em'.
That's how
I get down.
What separates
the playas'

272

from
The Players;
'IZ'
the clowns.

Dedicated to: *The best 'CLOWN ACT' in town coming to a circus near you.*

A B.A.D. Poem

Silhouettes

By: Author Renee' Drummond-Brown

*Two young
strangers
who
met.*

*They
told us
"get 'ov'r' it."*

*It's
simply
puppy 'luv'
yet.*

*Now
here we are
'sum'
40 years
later.
2
silhouettes
that
'neva' fade
in
the heat
of
the*

sweltering
(you guessed it)
Southern
shade.

Our silhouettes
covered
a
multitude
of sin.
Calypso-style.
Yeah,
we gave out
but
'neva'
gave in.
We gave our parents
a run
for their
monies.
But why?
They had
none.

They
told us
"get 'ov'r' it."

It's
simply

puppy 'luv'
yet.

Now
here we are
'sum'
40 years
later.
2
silhouettes
that
'neva' fade
in
the heat
of
the
sweltering
(you guessed it)
Southern
shade.

Our
Silhouettes
have
become
'ONE'.
In the
Eastern
(you guessed it)
'Son'.

They
told us
"get 'ov'r' it."

It's
simply
puppy 'luv'
yet.

Now
here we are
'sum'
40 years
later.
2
silhouettes
that
'neva'
fade
in
the heat
of
the
sweltering
(you guessed it)
Southern
shade.

Our silhouettes
replenished
tHIS

earth
(3 times though)
using
the garden
of
Edens
Northern
dirt.

They
told us
"get 'ov'r' it."

It's
simply
puppy 'luv'
yet.

Now
here we are
'sum'
40 years
later.
2
silhouettes
that
'neva' fade
in
the heat
of
the

sweltering
(you guessed it)
Southern
shade.

Our puppy
'luv'
shook them
to
the east;
shook
them
to the
West…

They
told us
"get 'ov'r' it."

It's
simply
puppy 'luv'
yet.

Now
here we are
'sum'
40 years
later.
2
silhouettes

that
'neva' fade
in
the heat
of
the
sweltering
(you guessed it)
Southern
shade.

And…when 'we'
say
our
final
good-bye's;
our
'SILHOUETTE'
will
fade
in the
sun
and
'jus' die
as
one.

Dedicated to: Shadows cast doubt.

A B.A.D. Poem

Skeleton's In Our Closet(S)

By: Author Renee' Drummond-Brown

Rib cage shown,
eyes bulging
from
the head;
'walkin'
on 2 sticks
'sum'

would call
legs
???
Saliva.
Foaming
at
the mouth.
Crust
in them eyes.
Death abounds.
Flies, flies, flies.
And more flies.
Yep,
thems' Moses
infamous plagues
everywhere!
The stench
of
debris.
A mother's plea;
nowhere
in sight.
A father
figure
who could
'NEVA'
be.

We 'CAN'T'
begin

to start
'wit dat'
man
in the mirror
cause
we're 'ALL'
about 'self'.
Blind
as a bat
an' don't
'wanna'
'SEE';
the Skeleton's
in our
'OWN'
Closet(S).
Beginning
'wit' me.

ALTERNATIVE POEM ENDING:
(Lord,
help me
to
help them,
and please
forgive me!)

Dedicated to: THE END.

A B.A.D. Poem

Slave Gal; Miss Mary Mack, Ain't got 'Nothin' On You!

By: Author Renee' Drummond-Brown

Miss slave gal
Brown, Brown, Brown.
'Wit' skin so
black, black, black.
An' 50
lashes, lashes, lashes.
Covering her 'WHOLE'
back, back, back.

She asked her
Massa, Massa, Massa.
To 'jus'
repent, repent, repent.
Before he
noosed her, noosed her, noosed her.
But 'NO' not
him, him, him.

He hung her
high, high, high.
She reached the
sky, sky, sky.
Cutting off 'ALL' oxygen
supply, supply, supply.
Slave gal hung her
head, head, head.
An' then she

died, died, died.
She couldn't come
back, back, back.
An' the onlookers
'NEVA'
cried, cried, cried!

Dedicated: *Someone call 911.*

A B.A.D. Poem

BARBARA SUEN

Barbara Suen is from Mishawaka, Indiana. She is 52. An age of wonder! Wondering where the "time" went after the busyness of raising three children and working. She enjoys writing prose poetry, and has been published in "Soul Fountain" and "The Storyteller" magazines. She has also been published in several poetry anthologies, of which she is very proud of. Her dream is to publish her own book of poetry! Like she tells her children, even now, "it all starts with a vision"!

"Special Reports In The Red"

By: Author Barbara Suen

"Special Reports In The Red"

Under Promises of Heaven
and threats of hell
in this angry world..."STOP"!
Special Report in a red box
Investigations, inside and out. All over.
Terror Attacks,
Travel Bans?
Missiles for who? What? Where?
Why?
Bombs in backpacks.
Innocence behind the fences, trapped,
and the hungry babies cry.
Too much spilled blood, in the rubble.
Did you turn away?
Clean Air, waters, land, pushed into the corner.
The "suit's" on the news... night and day.
I'm looking for the good news in vain.
I am sick in my whole being with the hatred and violence.

Always a "War."
Never any winners. Don't you see?
Not you.
Not them.
Not us.

It's "We the People"
Not "over" the people.
Have they forgotten?
You cannot change the Constitution. Ever.

Peace fighters lead,
don't follow!
March long and endlessly, hand in hand.
Lifting your voices loud and strong,
so loud, it reaches the heavens.

"Peace"!
For the people.
All people!

Even our "Lady of Liberty" cries in the night,
just like a mother who has lost her children.
She held the torch for so long, to light the way for all.
Those who were weary, and tired, searching for freedom.
Depite everything, our lady holds her torch higher now.
With strength, and hope.

Start with that "one" voice.
Let that voice be yours !

Jean C Bertrand from Haiti. A nature lover God-fearing. Using my poetry to bring peace and love in this place calling Earth.

Queens, NY

So thankful

By: Author Jean C Bertrand

So thankful
Borrow a laughter
From the sun
Open the door
Crying out the veins
Could not speak
There again found solace

So thankful
Borrow a dance
Long-nights in the forest
Learning the footsteps of life
Nights and days following the universe
The hidden flames gone with glee
Weeping gently while dancing with splendor

So thankful
Borrow a cup of divine rain
To cleanse the darken chamber
Rejuvenate that physical flesh
Shielding under the breath of holiness
Embracing life with its majestic grandeur
Dancing day and night rapturous delight

(C)2017
Jean C Bertrand

MS. JOY L. JOHNSON

Ms. Joy Johnson wrote this Prepositional Poem as part of an assignment for her Business English class. Ms. Johnson lives in Pittsburgh, Pennsylvania.

Stand!

By: Author Joy L. Johnson

Beyond the eventide,
Down by the riverside, I lie.
During the breeze, shadows of woes linger.
Before the dawn, slivers of melancholy approaches,
Above the Heaven, I gaze beyond the milky way.
Across the spiritual realm,
Under the shadow of God's wing, I am protected.
Between now and then, here and there,
Throughout the night I kneel and pray.
Beyond the Riverside, I stand!

Elizabeth "Betty"Asche Douglas, visual artist, musician and educator, earned a BFA degree in painting & design from Carnegie Mellon and an MA degree in Fine Arts from the University of Pittsburgh. She has done additional graduate work at the University of Pennsylvania. She has taught in high school and college, retiring as full professor from Geneva College in 1996. She is artist/owner of Douglas Art Gallery, Rochester, PA. Her professional exhibiting record covers over 5 decades, beginning with an award in the Associated Artists of Pittsburgh 42nd Annual at the Carnegie Museum. She has won numerous awards, including Jurors' Awards in the 64th Youngstown, OH, Area Artists Annual and the 2005 Appalachian Corridors Exhibition in Charleston, WV. In 2008 she was among 250 artists selected for an exhibition and catalog published to honor Pittsburgh's 250th anniversary. She was also one of 24 artists chosen statewide for the 2008-2010 traveling exhibition "Celebrating Visual Traditions, sponsored by the Pennsylvania Council on the Arts. In 2011 she was included in exhibitions at the American Jewish Museum, Pittsburgh and the African American Museum, Philadelphia, PA. In 2012 she showed at the August Wilson Center, Pittsburgh, The Southern Alleghenies Museum, Ligonier, PA and the African American Museum, Dallas, TX. From November 2013 through January 2014, her work was included in The New Collective at the Pittsburgh Center for the Arts. She was the featured artist in the 2014 Midland (PA) Arts Council's Summer Gallery. In 2015, her work was included in the Society of Sculptors 80th Anniversary show at Seton Hill U. Her works are in public and private collections in the U.S. and abroad. She has served as curator or juror for many art shows. She received the 2006 Service to the Arts Award from the Guild Council of the Pittsburgh Center for the Arts. She and her work have been featured in Carnegie Mellon Magazine, Christians in the Visual Arts Directory, Designing Home Lifestyles, Pittsburgh Magazine, Soul Pitt Quarterly and in the Beaver County Senior News. She has been profiled in The Beaver County and Allegheny Times and The New Pittsburgh Courier. In 2003, Geneva College honored her with a Tribute Banquet and Retrospective Exhibition to launch a fund in her name for a Geneva College Center for the Arts. She is archived in the National Museum of Women in the Arts and her biography is included in Marquis Publishing's *Who's Who in America*, *Who's Who of American Women*, *Who's Who in American Education* and *Who's Who in the World*. She is listed in Galey Publishing's *Who's Who Among African Americans* and in the International Biographical Centre, Cambridge, U. K. *Who's Who in the 21st Century* and *International Directory of Women in the Arts*. Around Beaver

County, where she is a Rochester resident, she is sometimes referred to as the "First Lady of the Arts." She serves on several boards of directors: Merrick Art Gallery Associates, Lincoln Park PerformingArts Charter School, Beaver Valley Local, American Federation of Musicians, the Midland Arts Council, and she is scholarship chair and former newsletter editor of the Rochester Chamber of Commerce. She is on the advisory board of Sweetwater Center for the Arts and the Guild Council of the Pittsburgh Center for the Arts. As "Betty Douglas," she performs as a vocalist and pianist in "Artistry in Song" and vocalist/leader with Betty Douglas & Co. She was inducted into the Beaver Valley Musicians' Hall of Fame in 2003. She has Internet pages on Facebook, the Pittsburgh Jazz Network and the Pittsburgh Live Music Network. She sings in the choir and is a soloist at St. Stephen's Church, Sewickley, PA. She also sings with the Incarnation Voices of the Anglican Incarnation Church, Pittsburgh. She does interactive lecture/performances in music and the visual arts for a wide variety of organizations and audiences.

Elizabeth "Betty"Asche Douglas
Douglas Art Gallery Artistry in Song
www.douglasartgallery.com
491 McKinley St, Rochester PA 15074
724-775-4618

Stand Your Ground

By: Author Elizabeth "Betty" Asche Douglas

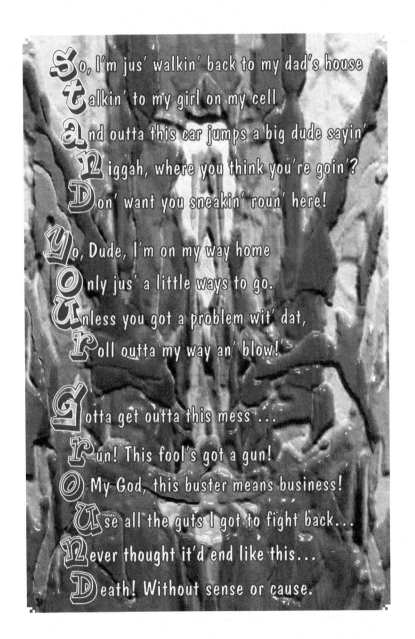

So, I'm jus' walkin' back to my dad's house

talkin' to my girl on my cell

and outta this car jumps a big dude sayin'

niggah, where you think you're goin'?

Don' want you sneakin' roun' here!

Yo, Dude, I'm on my way home

Only jus' a little ways to go.

Unless you got a problem wit' dat,

roll outta my way an' blow!

Gotta get outta this mess . . .

run! This fool's got a gun!

O My God, this buster means business!

Use all the guts I got to fight back . . .

Never thought it'd end like this . . .

Death! Without sense or cause.

Still I Write

(The Answer to: Dr. Maya Angelou's "Still I Rise")

By: Author Renee' Drummond-Brown

Maya,
Of course,
they wrote you down
in history,
You proved
them wrong
in truth,
But you
planted for me
calligraphy,
So,
I'm heard on paper
all the way
to God's celestial roof!

My passion for writing
does upset them,
But
I can't be
concerned,
Cause you
left for me
a gift from God,
And it'll be
forever
writing that I yearn.

Just like God's Raven
leaving the Ark,
'She' flew
to and fro,
Until the waters
were dried up
from off the earth.
Because of you,
I'll forever
write
in the skies,
seas
and dirt;
for certain
this
I do know.

I was
that broken soul,
And bowed
so low
to Satan's pit,
With nowhere
to get;
but up,
I allowed my pen
to place me
within God's Script (ure).

I know

my writings
excite you,
And with God
for you,
who can be
against us,
in giving me
that nod,
I finally hear
your words
loud and clear,
The poems you left behind
are messages
of truths,
minus
the facades.

Some have
shot my writings
to pieces,
While others
have damaged me
over time,
But God;
sends a ram
in a bush,
ink,
a quill,
and wrote for me
Ecclesiastes 3
He Author's

the time and place
with limited 'seasons'
for their
hurtful rhymes.

From the shame
you told me to write,
I write,
From the pain
you told me to write,
I write,
I am
that Raven Blackbird
with a large wingspan,
"Renee's Poems With Wings Are Words In Flight"
flying all over
God's land,
I too
want to leave behind
my unhealthy fears,
So,
in the dark,
I write,
But in the light,
I see
the imagery
our ancestors gave
to you;
which you
passed onto me,
Maya,

you are the dream,
Barack Obama
was the hope,
and I
am the slave set free
(to write).
Still I write,
I write,
I'll write.

Dedicated to: *A Tribute to Dr. Maya Angelou*

A B.A.D. Poem

Stop the Bus

By: Author Jean Morse

I get on and sit down.
My ride has started.
Looking out the window
at life
going by.

Not easy
looking at it;
what's that,
school - kids - marriage - work
good times - bad times.

One stop
left,
mines.

Stop the bus.

Strawberry Letter 23

By: Author Renee' Drummond-Brown

Where Beauty Lies
a mother's poem

Not the whispered wings of dragonflies
Nor the golden hues of sweet sunrise
Your lips, your cheeks, your nose, your eyes
This is where true beauty lies

Not the melodic charm of an ocean sigh
Nor a moonlit cloud in a starlit sky
Your dreams, your hopes, your laughs, your cries
This is where true beauty lies

Not the morning dance of a butterfly
Nor the soothing tune of a cricket's cry
Your heart, your soul, your love, your mind
This is where true beauty lies

I stand in wonder at all He did create
I stand in wonder at the beauty of your face
In a world full of splendor, I take no surprise
That nothing compares in a mother's eyes

Your 'luv'
'iz' raw.
It took her
by storm.
Caught her
off guard;
when you rained,
you poured.

But…
In the game
of 'luv';
often 'tymes'
They had to
go back
to start.
Could not
pass go.
For 'tymes'
such as these;
it
stunted
their growth…

But…
In spite
of it
all.
They held onto;
two separate worlds;
Strawberry Letter 23,
and
the 'ONE'
true
Living God.

Dedicated to: *LOVE conquers 'ALL' 'thangs'!!!*

A B.A.D. Poem

Stream of Thought

By: Author Renee' Drummond-Brown

*Stream of thought
is liken
to
wisdom
of
ancient
proverbs
an'
variations
of cultural
influences.
Why
does
one's
heart skip
a beat
with
palpitations
when
they
hear, see
and/or
speak
evil revelations.*

Wise
as a dove;
gentle
as a
serpent
with three
wise monkeys
on its back;
showing
'nadda'
love
to anyone,
with a
stream of thought
or
thereof
?

Dedicated to: *Watercourse.*

A B.A.D. Poem

'SUM' RIVERS RUN DEEP

By: Author Renee' Drummond-Brown

Does your river
run deep?
Like the bloodline
through
the grave.
Or
does
Satan
own
that soul?
Can
you be moved
by 'dawgz'
'anna'
water-hose
of the
60's movement?
Lord knows.
He knows.

Does your river
run deep?
Like the bloodline
through the grave.
Or
can you
be loyal
down
to the bone?
Lord knows.
He knows,
I SHALL NOT BE MOVED;
my river
runs~ ~ ~ ~
way
'TOO' deep.

Dedicated to: *Faithfulness*

A B.A.D. Poem

Survival of the Fittest

By: *Author Renee' Drummond-Brown*

*We need
you 'kidz'*

to survive.
Live life,
endure,
subsist,
hold-on.
Continue that
rat
race;
just
stay alive
in doing
what you do.

We know
'sum' 'thangs'
ain't
alright.
'Wee'z' be
'lyin'
to say
differently.
Like
a man blind
'wit'
20/20
hindsight.

Believe you
me.

We need
you
to survive.
If not
for self
then
someone
else.

Survive for:
our true
identity.
Survive for:
our true
history.
Survive for:
our
little
bitty babies
'makin' babies
an'
lest we forget
'dem'
hard-hard 'boyz'
'dyin'
in them
city
paved streets.
Survive for:
our legacy.

Survive not only
for you
but,
for me too!
Do
what you 'gotta' do
but
survive.
That be 'YOU'.

Odd
as it may seem;
The Father
made no junk.
No accidents;
justUS
peculiar
black beings.
We need
the
survival of the fittest
to
carry out
the ancestors
African dreams.
Carry-out
the hope
of the slave
WHO;
'jus'

like a King,
hung high
in 1619
on
Jamestown's
finest of finest
proficient trees.
JUST SURVIVE
PLEASE!

Dedicated to: *Slaves hung high, were stretched wide an' were born; to merely die.*

A B.A.D. Poem

'Takin' You For A Ride

By: Author Renee' Drummond-Brown

80
years old.
She
23.
He
'thinkin'
she's
in 'luv'
hmm;
she's after
HIS
MONEY.

80
years old.
She
23.
He
'thinkin'
he's
in 'luv'
hmm;
He's 'jus'
LONELY.

80
years old.
She
23.
'Takin''
him
for a ride;
like an'
ol''
pro
'witta'
street 'walkin''
history.

A young
man's
nightmare
'anna'
old man's
dream.
A young
lady
'witta'
woman's mind
DANGEROUS
as MJ would belt out an' sang!!!

'DATS'
'NOBODY'S'
baby.
She's
23
'takin' him for a ride
an' he's
too old
to
SEE.

Dedicated to: *A smooth criminal.*
Old men dream dreams while the young have nightmares.

A B.A.D. Poem

'Talkin' Head(s)

By: Author Renee' Drummond–Brown

Her head screws on
an' off.
You're out of her head man.
Once strung out;
its your loss.
She's so
vain;
he's so
lost
???

Dedicated to: *THIS POEM AIN'T 'BOUT' YOU!!!*

A B.A.D. Poem

The ?

By: Author Renee' Drummond-Brown

be to not or be To;
to be or not to be,
is the answer;
I question thee?

Dedicated to: 'IZ' the question; I ask of thee.

A B.A.D. Poem

The Battle of The Roses

By: Author Renee' Drummond-Brown

Someone said
*the **BLUE** rose*
reaches
the unattainable,
the impossible.
While,
CORAL
sparks

fires

to

one's

desire.

Nevertheless,

LAVENDER

finds

her 'luv'

at

the last

sight

of

enchantment.

Bet.

Then

LIGHT PINK

comes along

bringing

admiration

'inna'

sweet

sympathetic

sang

or

song

whichever

the case

may be.

ORANGE

enthusiasm

reaches

far beyond
her fascinations
of desires
to be set free.
But
one thang
for sure
PALE PEACH
has
'sum'
modesty
way beyond
her reach.
While
PEACH
has
gratitude
and
appreciates
that
PINK
has class,
style
an' yes
even grace
that
lives
within
perfect
happiness.
Love.

Is not

limited

to

the beauty,

the courage

the respect

that

defines

THE

RED ROSE.

But

'neva'

forget

THE RED ROSE BUD

for she's

symbolic

of

her

purity

an'

transparency

in

loveliness.

Yeah

that

might be me

(not sure though.)

RED AND WHITE

given together

is

a sure sign

of
unity's
plea.
WHITE
claims her
youthfulness,
purity
and yes
even
innocence.
In hindsight
The
WHITE
ROSEBUD
allegorically
is
a sign
of
girlhood.
Nevertheless,
YELLOW
'brangs'
joy.
An'
welcomes back
friends
both
far an' near.
However,
YELLOW WITH A RED TIP
is definitely

meant
to fall
head
'ov'r'
heels!

BUT…
I SAY…
ROSES AREN'T RED
AN'
VIOLETS
AIN'T
HARDLEY
BLUE…
THE BLACK ROSE…
YES
BLACK…
TRIUMPHS
AND SHE
BATTLES
THEM ALL
IN
TRUTH!

Dedicated to: *Best buds vs. the war of the **ROSES**.*

A B.A.D. Poem

The Ending

By: Author Renee' Drummond-Brown

*How you start off;
is how
you'll ultimately
end.
Now
pay close attention
to
that ending.
In hindsight,
you both
really
'neva'
began.*

Dedicated to: *Do not pass go.*

A B.A.D. Poem

Sweet Peace Marciana Collins is twelve years old. She was born in and still lives in Pittsburgh, Pennsylvania with her Mom, Dad, four siblings, two cats and one snake. She has never been afraid to raise her voice.

The Sound of My Voice
By: Author Sweet Peace Collins

The sound of my voice calls to the undead
Telling them to retreat

The sound of my voice calls to the volcanoes
Telling them to hibernate

The sound of my voice protests against
Police Brutality

The sound of my voice mimics Dr. Martin Luther King

The sound of my voice freezes time and
Everyone in it

Yet the sound of my voice is lost in
The wind forever

The Wild, Wild West

By: Author Renee' Drummond–Brown

My pen's
bad
as can be.
Shoots no blanks.
Cogitates
the
ink
she thINKS.

Shoots
2
to the head.
1
to the chest;
no questions
asked
no prisoner's
exempt.
You guessed
'WRITE';
the thINKing pen's
'sho' 'nuff'
blessed.

Writing's
my game,
creativity's
my 'thang'.
Poetry's
my signature name

an' 'YES'
trait!

Come at me
'betta'
come correct
at best;
cause
when I 'DRAW'
my gun
I INK
LIKE I'M IN
THE
Wild, Wild West!

You'll take two to the head
one to the chest;
my INKpen
slays
like a head hunter
at its best!

Dedicated to: *Duel fights take two and my INKpen will annihilate you!*

A B.A.D. Poem

There's 'NO PLACE' Like Home

By: Author Renee' Drummond-Brown

Abuse
is shown
fist
are thrown.
Lies
have grown
faces
are frowned.
Money stolen,
far
from a loan.
Absolutely
'NO LOVE'
shown.
Unwanted
babies born.
Click your heels
three times…
'An'
run away
(IF ONLY IN YOUR MIND)
fast as you can
'FROM'
home!

Dedicated to: 'Dem' kids 'livin' on 'dem' streets

A B.A.D. Poem

Hank Beukema was born in Woodbury, New Jersey, USA in 1951.

He now lives in Pomona, NY

He is a former musician and has worked for a major car company

much of his life. He crossed the country five times hitchhiking and has

many great stories. He has written poetry for many decades except for a twenty year pause for personal reasons. He has just retired and looking to do voice over and spoken word work in the future. His only son died 25 years ago and changed his life. He is also a recovering alcoholic with ten years clean.

THIS IS

By: Author Hank Beukema

This is the wallpaper in the tenement in Cleveland in 1954
This is an October Sunday at Yankee Stadium in 1976
This is everything you wished I was and everything I wished I wasn't
This is too hot to handle and too much to bare
This is all I held back that you needed
This is the love of a lifetime passing in the street
This is the letters I meant to write
This is all the I'm sorrys we never get to say
This is an aching deep inside from need
This is vanilla spice candles and the smell of cinnamon

This is tangible evidence of insanity
This is dancing crazy alone without being drunk
This is the poets trying to keep from drowning
This is the soldier who wonders why
This is seeing God in a woman's eyes and looking for it again forever
This is losing everything and starting over
This is playing music and hearing the crowd applauding
This is what it's come down to

This is perfect sex
This is postcoital postpartum postnasal depression
This is off the beaten path without a paddle
This is the side of the road with no destination
This is vanilla chocolate And strawberry

This is going to the grocery store hungry
This is running with the scissors just because you can
This is tipping your cap to Don Quixote
This is waiting for the Rapture in a black suit

This is a hundred thousand voices singing I can't get no satisfaction
This is blue eyes and brown eyes and redheads and blonds
This is the one who leaves you wanting and
The one you want to leave
This is an adult dose of the grownup's medicine
This is the beginning of the end of the beginning
This is re-creation, revelation, pain and frustration,
This is forgiveness and redemption
This is salvation, edification, sanctification….
Healing…

This is most of what you needed and a little of what you wanted
This is all you thought it would be
This is exactly as it should be
This is what you made it…

Yeah,
That's what This is…

THIS LAND IS RAVEN'S LAND

By: Author Renee' Drummond–Brown

That blackbird couldn't land,
to pluck from land;
olive leaf's off of the land
because she foresaw desert land,
inward lands,
"The Red Sea" in middle of the land,
the Black Holocaust land
intended for Indians land
cause history said this land
is your land
this land is my land
from the coast of California's land
to the New Stanton New York is~~~land.
No, 'twas not the doves land.
The Raven flew to and fro 'ov'r' no-man's land.

Dedicated to:
"And he sent forth a raven,
which went forth to and fro,
until the waters
were dried up from off the earth"
(Genesis 8:7 KJV).

A B.A.D. poem

NANCY NDEKE

Name:
Nancy Ndeke
Nationality:
Kenyan.
Residence:
Nairobi.
Career:
Teacher for two decade's
Consultant on conflict management with Multimedia consultant (Nairobi).
OTHERS
Child protection services.
Gender equality's sensitization activities.
Theater and drama artist
Author
Poet
And mother.

TIME THAT CALL GOD.

By: Author Nancy Ndeke

It's OK
To rant and rave
Question the way
Frown on the day
Set aside the deity
Drunk with health
Drenched in wealth.
It's OK
With a full purpose
And a drunken curse
To swim in pass
Laughing with crass
Stout with class
Defending wrong
Denying Deity.
It's OK
You who know the why
The choice he weighed
To follow his ways
Beyond our whims
And when on bedded knees
We renounce ourselves
We take piece's to peace.
It's OK
To look and hear
The up and down
Of world of man

Who daily write
His rules to rule
And shun the sage
And records of right
Embracing own.
What's not OK
Is crime of war
It's drive of battle
It's demise of moral
It's death of child
It's sale of other
It's rob of livelihood
It's engineered hunger
It's doctored poverty
It's schemed sickness
It's skewed teaching
For then you be
A god of change
A change that hurts
Creators creatures
And Lol!!!!
Believe it or not
There shall be charges to answer
Some day!!!!!.

Today, Tomorrow and Always

By: Author Renee' Drummond–Brown

Today,
I'm here
protecting you.
Tomorrow,
I may be gone
way
too soon.
In your future(s)
journey-on;
in the
'VERY SAME'
fashion
as
B.A.D.'s
prophetic songs.
Remember,
change nothing
but
pass those songs
onto
your
children's
children
children's
children

to
carry
on;
looong,
loooong,
looooong
after
I'm gone.

Dedicated to:
I'll sing a song for you~ ~ ~ RocDeeRay~ ~ ~ **Today, Tomorrow and Always.**

"TRUTHS" (POEM)

Role your eyes
click your lips;
you are just a teenage spince.
Now, you're grown
on your own.
Think of your mom
being alone!
Didn't mean to fuss;
didn't mean to act
tough
but
we both started a fight.
So,
here's the truth
I was wrong;
and so
were you,
so
let's get over it
&
then
we both
call it truths.

This poem was given to me by my 'little' daughter and namesake, Renee' Barbara-Ann Brown, many, many, many moons ago!

"TRUTHS" ANSWER

By: Author Renee' Drummond-Brown

The eyes
you rolled
and…
The smack of your lips;
I prayed silently
at
your teenage spince.

Now
you are grown
but never alone
thanks to The Father;
He's been there
from birth!
Mom knew who to lean on
and only in Him,
did I trust;
now
you understand
that agape love
shared tween' Christ
and
the both
of us.

Your right was wrong and my wrong was right.
AND SO WHAT
 you frowned.
Look at God.
He ALONE
produced:
Dr. Renee' Barbara-Ann Brown

(Congratulations WVU Graduate-Class of 2017)

UNEDUCATED, UNINFORMED, IGNORANT, UNSCHOOLED, UNTRAINED FOOLS!

By: Author Renee' Drummond-Brown

They don't like you
if
you're on the dope.
They don't like you
if
you don't smoke.
They don't like you
if
you're way too loud.
They don't like you
if
you don't
entertain their crowd.
They don't like you
if
you live
quiet,
meek an' proud.
They don't like you
if
you have
a house.
They don't like you
if
you don't
own a couch.

And they certainly
don't like you
if
you're a Father fearing church mouse.
They don't like you
if
you stay to yourself.
They don't like you
if
you're with someone else.
They don't like you
if
you mind
your business.
They don't like you
if
you're always
'inna' mess.
They don't like you
Anyhow…
SO,
DARE TO BE DIFFRERENT
AND LEAVE ALONE
THE LIKES
OF THEIR ILLITERATE
KIND(s)!!!

Dedicated to: *Stupid is as stupid does and yes, that glove fits you; down to the thumb.*

A B.A.D. Poem

UnSPOKEN Word

By: Author Renee' Drummond-Brown

The best writers
writing prose
are his
and/or
her thoughts;
that
no-one
else
could
'EVER'
know.

They are
one's
most
private parts~~~ inner thoughts;
'NOT'
written
on papyrus,
but rather
carried out
in one's
rhythmic
heart.

Dedicated to:
$hhhhh…quiet on the set, please. God is 'tryin' to tell 'ME' 'sumthin' (right now!)

A B.A.D. Poem

USER'S

By: Author Renee' Drummond-Brown

Funny how
we
'AIN'T'
family
foe
nor
friend;
'UNTIL',
your 'legal' troubles
begin.
'THEN'
Hun,
we're one
for all.
'AND'
all
for one
my 'KIN'!

Dedicated to: *What have you done for me lately?*

A B.A.D. Poem

WAR. What Is It Good For? 'EVERYTHANG'!

By: Author Renee' Drummond-Brown

I declare war

on

my oppressors.

I declare war

on

the lessor

of

two evils.

I declare war

on

my

persecutors.

I declare war

on

child molesters.

I declare war

on

hate crimes.

I declare war

on

hard times.

I declare war

on

enemy lines.

I declare war

on

un-just

bias.
I declare war
on
drug dealers
pimps
prostitutes
and
liars.
I declare war
on
Satan's hire.

God ain't
'comin' back
to 'brang'
no peace;
He's 'comin' back
with a vengeance
to finally
'FREE'
his peeps.
WAR.
What Is It Good For?
'EVERYTHANG'
WRONG
as you
can'SEE'.

'WATCH' The Vultures

By: Author Renee' Drummond-Brown

Long
after
I'm gone.
My books
will
sail on;
for your
benefit(s).

Way after
my death;
for me,
my children
will
walk
THE RED CARPET.
They just
don't
cogitate it
yet!

I've read into
their future(s)
long
after
I'm gone.
My prolific prose
will
soar,
carry on
and

my
children's children's children
will be
in awe.

But
when gone…
don't weep for me!
Cause finally,
I'll be
set free
to write~~
You guessed,
'sum'
inexhaustible
poetry.

YEAH,
the best
of my best
un-seen
un-spoken
un-heard of;
productive
work
yet!!!

BUT…
My children
remember to
'WATCH'
the vultures
circling
your
door-step(s)
as you
sojourn on.

Dedicated to: *Hidden Figures~~~SHHH-"RocDeeRay"*
A B.A.D. Poem

Weed

By: Author Renee' Drummond-Brown

Sow a seed
Plant a tree
Water 'n' 'Son'
Reap the growth
Leave it be
Fend for self
Watch the weed
Cocoon
A
Tree

Dedicated to: *Wildflower's*

A B.A.D. Poem

What Do I 'SEE'?

By: Author Renee' Drummond-Brown

'Lookin'
out the window;
what
do I see?
I 'SEE'
depravation,
retaliation
discrimination
an'
racism
peering in
on me.

'Lookin'
in
my mind;
what
do I see?
I 'SEE'
a battlefield
which cogitates
the plagues
and their
ability
to get
at thee.

'Lookin'
in
my heart;
what
do I see?
I 'SEE'
submissiveness
in a world
that
won't let
one
be.

Yeah,
I 'SEE'
all things
in a world
who's lost
her true
identity.

That for sure
is what
I
'SEE'.

Dedicated to: *Stop, look an' listen to THEE.*

A B.A.D. Poem

Author Deborah Brooks Langford

Deborah is a mother, grandmother, and wife of many years. A Child of the King Jesus!
Deborah is from Gastonia, North Carolina.
She is a published Author of Forty-Seven Books.
You can find her on Lulu, Amazon, Barnes and Noble.

What's Right (Poem)

By: Author Deborah Brooks Langford

My goodness what is right anymore?
Is it right to be happy
Is it right to laugh or to be loved?
Is it right to cry what about heartache?
Is it right to die?
Or is that the only thing we can do right?

I heard the other day that we have no rights to do anything
I heard about the pain, the bullets no gain
I heard about unfulfilled dreams
How can I comprehend and now its gone?

What's right do you know?
It used to be love and hugs
Lots of lollipops
Beautiful dreams of white picket fences
With beautiful flowers lined in a roll

Now its guns and hate
Lying in tears
Rolled up in the grass
Hiding from haters.

Find the right in our Lord.
Only right to know is our Jesus
He will spread out the red carpet of roses
For your little feet

'O Lord we beseeched thee
Show the world what's right
Make our lights shine one more time.'

Looking out from the mountains
Overlooking the ocean
Through the prairie flat lands
To the beautiful valleys
Let's look to see what is right.

Hearts that are tender
Please don't make them bleed
Let them smell the roses
Let them know what's right.

DENISE BASKERVILLE

Denise Baskerville-MSW - Master Social Work

Born: Atlanta Ga. USA

Author: Destiny's Secret - Spiritual Poetry/Blog

Profession: Life Counselor, Writer, Poet Play-Wright, Social Activist, Mother, Grandmother

Spiritual Manifesto: I believe our greatest gifts are not wrapped in ribbons or bows. The promise, purpose and passion is hidden in pain, torment, and sorrow. When we apply wisdom, faith, and tears, to our deepest fears, adversity, and circumstances, we water the ground, thus the dry bones, dry places, can live again; we can rise up out of the ashes of indifference and become the man or woman God has destined us to be.

WHISPERS

Written by: Denise Baskerville

the whispers torment my mind
how do I know if it is God Divine
eternity is Destiny beyond the grave
the voices in my head refuse to behave
as I write prose & verse
Is this a gift or is it a curse!
enslaved by my spiritual pen
I kneel to the whispers deep within

Whispers that scream

Written by: Renee' Drummond-Brown

Within destiny's
deepest whispers
'her' pen
secretly screams
"INK the vision"
an' then
rehearse.
'She' makes it plain
so, others will run
to read 'her' worth.
Free at last; free at last;
which is worse?
The way a king thinks
or
'her' mind tormented of whispers turned into screams
of 'her'
black splattered INK?

Dedicated to my Poetic Sister: Denise Baskerville
c/oDestiny's Secret©2017 Spiritual Poetry®

AUTHOR SHAHID ABBAS

Author Shahid Abbas is from the City of Tandlianwala Punjab, which is in the District of Faisalabad, Punjab, Pakistan and he thoroughly enjoys writing poetry in his spare time on various social forums.

Who am I???

By: Author Shahid Abbas

I've ruined myself, yet I'm alive.
I've protected myself, yet I'm dead
My life is full of uncertainty
Now a fear is in my sphere,
Am I dead or alive?

Life is claiming you are mine
Death is warning you are not
I question myself,
Who am I?
I'm nothing; No! I'm nothing

My soul is wandering here and there
Tell me, who am I?
Why am I trapped in certain fears.
Who am I?
Should I exist or not?
That is fear in my sphere.

WHOOP, WHOOP, WHOOOP!

By: Author Renee' Drummond-Brown

'Jus'
got their
news;
'havin'
'TWINS'!
'Everythangs'
bout to be
bought,
two
by twos.
One

in pink.
One
in blue.
He quickly
drove home
to share
his
infallible news.
Sirens
pull 'em'
'ov'r'.
Lights 'flashin'
Red' 'WHITE' & blue!!!
Pow.
Pow.
Pow.
Pow.
Pow.
Pow.
Pow.
All
that's left
are twins
he
never knew
??

Dedicated to: *Another one bites the dust...* **and another one of us 'GONE'.**

A B.A.D. Poem

Who's BAD?

By: Author Renee' Drummond-Brown

Don't you blink.
Like
MJ;
my prose
is
'BAD'
as
can be.
When
I come on the scene
I'll
right the wrongs
before
one
can think.

Who's bad?
You know
I'm bad.
As can be.
…AND
I
DON'T
COME
OUT;
UNLESS,
I
CAN
INK!

Dedicated to: *Who's BAD? You 'know' I'm bad!*

A B.A.D. Poem

Witness Protection

By: Author Renee' Drummond-Brown

Say 'sumthin'
to me
or
mine(s)
and
you'll
'SEE'
A lioness
come out
of
retirement;

to tear up
'legally'
the likes
of your
kind.

Make
no mistakes,
I 'WILL'
lay
my life down
for
RocDeeRay
on any
given
Sunday.

Dedicated to: *My children.*

"Greater love hath no man than this, that a man lay down his life
for his friends" John 15:13 King James Version (KJV)

THAT'S LOVE!!!

A B.A.D. Poem

You and I

By: Author Renee' Drummond-Brown

Slick Rick
said
we'd be together
til'
the six
was nine.
You said

I was fine
as wine.
Society said
they'll be threw
just give it
some time.
Momma said
that kind of love
has
no reason
nor rhyme.
Daddy said
I don't like
the likes
of his kind.
Friends say
he ain't
your type.

Well guess what
naysayers?
The six
still ain't
nine!!!

Dedicated to: *You can't hurry love*

A B.A.D. Poem

You Can't Serve Two Trees; You 'MUST' Love One and Hate the Other!

By: Author Renee' Drummond-Brown

The 'TREE'
of life
has
THE
POWER
of oxygen
to make one
breath.

~~~~

AND

~~~~

them
'Southern' trees
have
the power
of death
to make one
swing.

You
can't serve
two trees;
you must
love one
TREE
and hate
the other
tree.

Where are you rooted
with
THEE
Or
thee?

Dedicated to: *Stand your ground.*

A B.A.D. Poem

'YOU' Don't Know Her Story

By: Author Renee' Drummond-Brown

She lays awake
at night.
She writes.
She hurts.
She pains.
She thinks
inside.
She's wise
beyond measure.
She sees
'ALL'
and knows;
'YOU'
don't know
her story.

Dedicated to: *She*

A B.A.D. Poem

YOU DON'T KNOW MY NAME

By: Author Renee' Drummond-Brown

Recall
my name
in
the dewdrops.
I'm not
be-gone.
I'm here,
springing high
with
hopes an' dreams
not questioning
who, what, when, where
or 'ev'n'
why?
Yet, sometimes how.

Rest assure
love is not here.
It's nowhere.
I remembered that,
an' then,
my hour slips by
an'
tell tale
signs
whispers
goodbye.

Dedicated to: *My descendants*

A B.A.D. Poem

Young, Gifted and Black!

By: Author Renee' Drummond-Brown

Until,
off
to college
you go,
an'
accurately
'SEE'
Professors
teaching
you
to be
all
you
can be.
And
suddenly!
You
realize
walking
SUMMA CUM LAUDE;
'YOU'
all along
were
Young, Gifted and Black
too.

'CEPT'...

'Nadda'
teacher
'NEVER'
noticed
and/or
told
you
'THAT'
throughout
school
???

Then
and
only then,
you realize;
'ALL'
odds
were
'ALWAYS'
betted
'AGAINST'
You!

Dedicated to: *A, B, C easy as 1, 2, 3.*

A B.A.D. Poem

Your Begin Will Define Your End

By: Author Renee' Drummond-Brown

The end.
Defines
one's
begin.
One's begin.
Defines
their
end.
How you start
out
with him
my friend;
is how
you'll
ultimately
end.
In hindsight,
thinking
back;
at
the
very
begin…

The relationship
was
already
at
its end.

Dedicated to: *THE END.*

A B.A.D. Poem

You're Drugged!

By: Author Renee' Drummond-Brown

Dreaming
of
the day;
everyone else
can change
to see
things
your delusional
way(s)!

Right
now!
Right now!!
You want it
Right now;
while everyone
else,
to you,
must
take a back seat
an' bow
down!
Yes down!!

Ugliness
an' useless
has become
your trademark.
It's everyone else's
fault
that you
in fact
never finish
what
you
in fact
start!

Greed
gets you
what
you want.
Everyone else
must pay
your cost
for you
to be
top shelf
boss.

Selfish
is who
you've
become;
with a
monkey
on your back.
taken
something ' for' nothing
while being
second
to
none!!!
AND I MEAN
TO
NO-ONE!!!

Dedicated to: *How you like me now MOMMA?*

A B.A.D. Poem

NEETU VAID SHARMA

Neetu Vaid Sharma is a poetess from Jalandhar City, India. Assistant Professor in English Literature for a decade, she has invested her immediate interest in writing. Being a passionate poet, she endeavours to reflect her intimate emotions through her book "PASSIONATE PLEASURE PEARLS." Her poems chiefly voice never dying love, basic instincts and storm of emotions occurring unpredictably in the journey of life. She has penned more than one hundred poems to her credit. Though had she tried her hand in short story writing and handful of essays, her crowning taste lies in poetry genre only.

ZILLION THUMPS UP

By: Author Neetu Vaid Sharma

FOR FRUITY POETRY

Flavours are flaunting to and fro
Testers losing brilliant taste
Where is that sumptuous dish
To be sensually relished by
Classics as well Romantics

Let this poetry get
A privileged place at
The most prestigious coffee tables of
Sophisticated book lovers
And be everlasting fruit fudge
On the lavish literary menu booklet
To match and meet
Choices of contemporary and old

Freshly fruit filled poetry must have
Banana's evergreen annually available appeal
Apple's appetizing attitude to ace all
Cherry's cheeriness to cheer one and all
Watermelon's water to wash worries
Grape's effortlessness – just pick and go for it
Papaya's anti diabetic relief cure
Mango's tempting miracle, luring young and old
Last but surely not the least
Pineapple's succulence for
Both the sweet and the sour
Along with the taste buds of fellow fruits

May this poetry be the most
Irresistible item to inquire about ever!

BIOGRAPHY

Renee' Drummond-Brown is an accomplished poetess with experience in creative writing. She is a (Summa Cum Laude) graduate of Geneva College of Western Pennsylvania and graduate of The Center for Urban Biblical Ministry (CUBM). Renee' is still in pursuit of excellence towards her mark for higher education.

She is working on her seventh book and has numerous works published globally which can be seen in cubm.org/news, KWEE Magazine (Liberian L. Review), Leaves of Ink Magazine, New Pittsburgh Courier, Raven Cage Poetry and Prose Ezine, Realistic Poetry International, Scarlet Leaf Publishing House, SickLit Magazine, The Metro Gazette Publishing Company, Inc., Tuck, Whispers and Wildfire Publications Magazine just to name a few.

Civil Rights Activist, Ms. Rutha Mae Harris, Original Freedom Singer of the Civil Rights Movement, was responsible for having Drummond-Brown's very first poem published in the Metro Gazette Publishing Company, Inc., in Albany, GA. Renee' also has poetry published in several anthologies and honorable mentions to her credit in various writing outlets. The Multicultural Student Services Office of Geneva College presented her with 2nd prize in the Undergraduate Essay Contest. Renee' also won and/or placed in several poetry contests globally. Several of her books were up for nomination and confirmed in the United Brothers United Sisters (UBUS) 2017, Black Book Awards for Excellence in Black Literature, held at the Nat Turner Library in Southampton County, Virginia.

She was Poet of the Month Winner in both Our Poetry Archives and Wildfire Publications Magazine, 2017, and in the prestigious Potpourri Poets/Artists Writing Community, 2016. The author has been interviewed by Urban Heroes Blog Talk Radio and her poetry aired on Fifth Wall Radio. She has even graced the cover of KWEE Magazine in the month of May, 2016. Her love for creative writing is undoubtedly displayed through her very unique style and her work solidifies her as a force to be reckoned with in the literary world of poetry. Renee' is inspired by non-other than Dr. Maya Angelou, and because of her, Renee' posits "Still I write, I write, and I'll write!"

Dedicated to: RocDeeRay

CPSIA information can be obtained
at www.ICGtesting.com
Printed in the USA
LVOW06s0630211217
560430LV00026B/1230/P